# The Mexican American Family:
Tradition and Change

# THE REYNOLDS SERIES IN SOCIOLOGY

Larry T. Reynolds, *Editor*

by **GENERAL HALL, INC.**

# The Mexican American Family:

## Tradition and Change

**Norma Williams**

*University of North Texas*

**GENERAL HALL, INC.**

*Publishers*

5 Talon Way

Dix Hills, New York 11746

The Mexican American Family:
Tradition and Change

GENERAL HALL, INC.
5 Talon Way
Dix Hills, New York 11746

Publisher: Ravi Mehra
Consulting Editor: Anand Sinha
Composition: *Graphics Division,* General Hall, Inc.

LIBRARY OF CONGRESS CATALOG CARD NUMBER: **89–82581**

ISBN: 0–930390–25–3 [paper]
      0–930390–26–1 [cloth]

**Manufactured in the United States of America**

Para mi familia:
Mis padres, Lupita y Allen Williams,
mis hermanas, Peggy y Laura, y hermanos,
Russell, Richard (Red), y Allen, Jr.

To my family:
My parents, Lupita and Allen Williams,
my sisters, Peggy  and Laura, and brothers,
Russell, Richard (Red), and Allen, Jr.

# Contents

**Acknowledgments**                                                          **ix**

## 1  Introduction                                                            1

Who Are the Mexican Americans? 2, Mexican Americans and U.S. Society
4, The Research Process 7, Specific Objectives 9, General Objectives 12,
Analysis of the Data and Presentation of the Findings 14, Notes 16

## 2  Traditional Life-cycle Rituals among Mexican Americans in Texas         18

The Social Significance of Life-cycle Rituals 18, The Nature of Tradition
among Mexican Americans 19, Rituals, Tradition, and Sacred Time 19, Tradition among Mexican Americans 20, The Religious Context 22, The Birth
Ceremony 23, The Marriage Ceremony 27, The Funeral Ceremony 33, Conclusions 38, Notes 39

## 3  Changes in Life-cycle Rituals and Family Life within the Working Class  41

Background Considerations 41, Generational Differences 42, The Nature of
Religion 43, The Baptismal Ceremony 44, The Marriage Rite 51, Funerals 56,
Conclusions 63, Notes 63

## 4  Changes in Life-cycle Rituals and Family Life within the Business and Professional class   64

Background Considerations 64, The Baptismal Ceremony 65, The Marriage
Rite 70, Funerals 74, Conclusions 80, Notes 82

## 5  Role Making and Decision Making within the Working Class                83

Perceptions of Change Over Time 84, Sex-role Expectations 87, Role Making
by Husbands and Wives: A Clarification of Issues 89, Specific Role-making

Patterns 90, Type I: A Personal (but Limited Social) Identity 92, Type II: An Emerging Personal and Social Identity 92, Type III: A Personal and Social Identity (with Reservations) 94, Resistance to Role Making 95, The Decision-making Process: Clarification of the Issues 96, Specific Decision-making Areas 97, Management of Finances 98, Purchase of a Car 99, Responsibility for House Repairs 101, Purchase of Furniture 102, Choice of Friends 104, Disciplining of Children 105, Conclusions 108, Notes 108

## 6 Role Making and Decision Making within the Professional Class 110

Perceptions of Change Over Time 111, Sex-role Expectations 113, The Role-making Process 115, Type I. The Reluctant Dependent 117, Type II. Semi-independent, Family Oriented 118, Type III. Semi-independent, Career Oriented 120, Type IV. Independent, with Constraints 121, Constraints on Role Making 121, The Decision-making Process 123, Management of Finances 124, Purchase of a Car 126, Responsibility for House Repairs 128, Purchase of Furniture 128, Choice of Friends 130, Disciplining of Children 132, Conclusions 134

## 7 Conclusions and Implications 136

Empirical Findings 136, Rethinking Theoretical Issues in the Study of the Family 140, Revisions in Symbolic Interaction Theory 140, Ethnicity 144, An Alternative to the Assimilationist Model 148, Concluding Remarks 150, Notes 151

## Appendix
## A Methodological Note 152

Data Collection 152, In-depth interviews 152, Participant Observation 156, The Objectifying Interview 157, The Researcher as Insider and Outsider 158, Analysis of the Data 159

## References 160

## Index 167

# ACKNOWLEDGMENTS

This book presents data on recent changes in the extended and conjugal family arrangements in the Mexican American working and professional classes. It represents the culmination of long-standing fieldwork in Austin, Corpus Christi, and the Kingsville region of Texas. The book is designed to be read by scholars and students alike.

I did all my own field research. But I could never have carried out this project without the assistance of numerous Mexican Americans. I am grateful to those persons who took the time to introduce me to respondents in Austin and Corpus Christi. Most important, I am deeply indebted to my respondents for their generosity in providing me with data about their lives. Inasmuch as I assured them anonymity, I am unable to thank them by name. They were extremely cooperative, and their support made my fieldwork an exciting and memorable experience.

I sincerely hope that this book will in some small way repay my respondents for their willingness to spend endless hours with me. As I have written articles and presented papers at numerous meetings, I have come to realize that many social scientists lack basic knowledge about Mexican Americans — the second largest minority group in the United States. In view of this, I hope the readers of this volume will gain a greater understanding and appreciation for the culture and lives of Mexican Americans.

Also, I wish to thank persons who commented on my earlier writings (parts of which have found their way into this book), and I have greatly profited from feedback from those who have read the book manuscript (or sections of it). These persons include Joan Moore, Vicki L. Ruiz, Mary Jo Deegan, Rodolfo Alvarez, Edna Hinojosa, Benigno Aguirre, Gloria Contreras, Cruz C. Torres, Barbara Finlay, Letticia Galindo, Diana Bustamante, Roberto Garza, Victor Arizpe, Irene Rodriguez, David Hinojosa, Naida Soliz, Esther Bonilla Read, Juanita B. Ortega Necer, Cecilia Garza, Dianna Densmore, Lisa (L.J.) Jordon, and Roel (Roy) Hinojosa. Jackie Sandles was most helpful in typing the revisions of the final drafts of this book.

The editorial assistance of Jane Sell and Andree Sjoberg has been especially valuable. Andree Sjoberg's careful attention to detail has been crucial in shaping the manuscript into book form. In addition, Gideon Sjoberg has been persistent in pushing me to upgrade my theoretical perspective, and he has suggested ways of integrating my theoretical analysis with the data I collected. Sociologists often talk about the interaction of theory and data, but this remains one of the most difficult aspects of the research process.

I also thank the College of Liberal Arts, Texas A&M University, for research support that permitted me to carry out fieldwork in Corpus Christi during the summer of 1985. I am especially grateful to the National Science Foundation/Minority Research Initiation Program (Document No. RII-8509893) for funding my research proposal. The grant supported research in Corpus Christi for two months during the academic years 1985-86 and 1986-87 and full-time fieldwork during the summer of 1986.

The NTL Institute has kindly permitted me to use selected materials from the article I published in the *Journal of Applied Behavioral Science* 24, no. 2, (1988).

Certain friends who have always encouraged me to pursue research on the Mexican American culture cannot go unmentioned. They are Dolores Davila-Medrano, Susana Mathis, Lionel Maldonado, Rebecca Sanchez-Orozco, Nilda L. Garcia, Stanley Bittinger, Robert Medrano, Maria Barrera, Jerry Bogener, Jackie Webb, and David Zufelt. In addition, I must acknowledge the assistance of my parents' friends who made many helpful suggestions during the different stages of this research.

I have dedicated this book *para mi familia—mis padres, hermanas y hermanos.* I admire my parents, who sacrificed in order to make life better for their children. They were insistent that all of us complete high school, and my mother was an active agent in intervening with the school system to assist us in securing fairer treatment than would otherwise have been the case.

I must also single out my sister, Laura, for special attention. In recent years she has taken on the difficult task of taking care of our parents, who suffered some serious health problems while I was working on this book. Despite her own family responsibilities, Laura was always there to offer her assistance to our parents. If she had not done so, it would have been very difficult for me to complete this book. "Laura, I am glad you are my sister and my dearest friend."


Norma Williams
University of North Texas
January, 1990

# Chapter 1    INTRODUCTION

This study fills a major void in our knowledge regarding contemporary family patterns among Mexican Americans, the second largest minority group in the United States. Although in recent years social scientists have demonstrated increased interest in the Mexican American family, no systematic study as yet exists regarding the changes that have occurred within the extended and conjugal family arrangements. A variety of research reports relying on social surveys and census data have appeared.[1] Although admittedly useful, they provide us with little understanding about the dynamics of family life in contemporary urban settings. Some studies within the qualitative tradition have focused on selected aspects of the Mexican American family. An informative work of this genre is that by Zavella (1987), who studied women cannery workers and demonstrated the impact that their work patterns have on their family arrangements. Nevertheless, no one has taken a more holistic perspective and examined the shifts within the extended family as well as in the relationships between husbands and wives in the conjugal family system. I seek to do so and in the process take into account the way in which Mexican Americans are, in the context of rapid social change, redefining their roles within the extended and conjugal families.

Many social scientists continue to generalize about the Mexican American family on the basis of research conducted several decades ago (see Queen et al. 1985). Primarily they rely on the research findings of anthropologists such as Madsen (1964), Rubel (1966), and Clark (1959). Madsen and Rubel carried out their research in small towns of South Texas a number of decades ago. Although their efforts continue to serve as the basis for generalizing about the Mexican American family, they are subject to serious criticisms.

From the perspective of the present, one obvious limitation of the research by Rubel and Madsen is that they were writing about life in small towns, and nowadays most Mexican Americans live in urban centers. To discuss Mexican Americans without taking cognizance of the major upheavals of the past several decades is to ignore certain basic realities. Moreover, Madsen and Rubel did not examine a number of features of family life discussed in the present volume.

Another weakness of the works of Madsen and Rubel relates to the stereotypes that they perpetuated. Paredes (1977), a noted folklorist, con-

1

tends that Rubel did not understand the idioms of the culture he was study-ing. Other social scientists have challenged the stereotypical views that Madsen and Rubel held of men and women (e.g., Baca Zinn 1975, 1982; Mirandé 1985).[2] Wives and daughters were perceived as passive and totally accepting of the husband's or father's authority. The man was characterized by his "machismo," or dominance over women. It seems apparent that, at least to some degree, Madsen and Rubel adopted the stereotypical definitions of the majority society in describing Mexican Americans. Of course they were not alone in this regard; their research was conducted before social scientists began reevaluating the role of women in traditional societies. It is more difficult to account for the observations of Horowitz (1983). She has perpetuated, based on her research in Chicago, some of the major distor-tions of men's and women's roles among Mexican Americans. Yet her work was written well after scholars had documented the lack of passivity of women, particularly in the private sphere, in a variety of cultural settings.[3] Since the 1970s, a sizable body of literature stresses that women in most societies have had a major influence in the "private," if not the "public," sphere (Rosaldo 1974).[4] The influence of women, especially within the home, has been shown to be much greater than previously assumed (e.g., Smith and Wiswell 1982).[5]

Although I am critical of the work of Rubel, Madsen, and Horowitz, for example, it would be unfair to ignore all the descriptive data that these scholars have amassed. We must, however, exercise care when interpreting their findings and must take account of the theory and research relating to the role of husbands and wives in other cultural settings.

## Who Are the Mexican Americans?

Many persons, including social scientists, have difficulty in defining who are Mexican Americans. If we look back at the history of how these persons have been defined in U.S. censuses, we find major shifts in the of-ficial labeling of this ethnic group by the federal government (Moore 1976). Nowadays, Mexican Americans are often confused with undocumented workers or with Mexican nationals. But their identity is different from that of either group.[6] In this book I use the term *Mexican American* rather than *Chicano;* however, the terms are synonymous.[7]

People of Mexican or Spanish heritage settled in the Southwest long before the Anglos arrived. In 1836 some of these persons were incorporated into the Republic of Texas. Then, following the Treaty of Guadalupe Hidalgo (1848) between Mexico and the United States, large sectors of the Southwest – Texas, New Mexico, Arizona, California, etc. – became part of the United States. People of Mexican heritage who lived within the newly incorporated political region were granted U.S. citizenship and the right to retain their property. But many Mexican Americans soon lost their lands to the newly arrived Anglos, who employed legal or fraudulent means in the process. This pattern was one feature of the discrimination that resulted in Mexican Americans becoming socially and economically disadvantaged citizens throughout the Southwest.

What should be emphasized is that numerous Mexican Americans in the Southwest trace their heritage back to the time when Mexico ceded land to the United States. Yet we should also recognize that even in 1848, important regional differences existed. Many Spanish speakers in New Mexico, for instance, trace their roots back to settlers of Spanish heritage in the 1500s and thus differ from other groups in the Southwest. Since that time, the cultural situation has become more complex because of the several waves of immigration from Mexico into the United States. According to Chavez (1984:31), Mexicans who migrated to the United States formed a steadily increasing stream that finally became a mass movement in the twentieth century. This flow of undocumented workers appears to have been especially heavy in the 1970s and 1980s (Bean and Tienda 1987).

The undocumented workers from Mexico have captured the attention of the mass media. Although some return to Mexico, others remain in the United States and become absorbed into the Mexican American cultural heritage. Moreover, these immigrants have settled not only in Mexican American communities in the Southwest but also throughout many parts of the West and Midwest. The ongoing immigration has contributed to the maintenance of the Spanish language and has shaped the Mexican American culture in the United States, but these immigrants, it must be emphasized, have in turn been shaped by the Mexican American culture of which they have become a part. They are Mexican Americans, not Mexicans.

Another major source of confusion in defining Mexican Americans is that they are assumed to be culturally like residents of Mexico. A number of social scientists have contributed to this definition of the situation.[8] Such an assumption fails to recognize that the political border between these two nations has had a major impact on shaping the Mexican American culture. While anyone who has lived in the border region between these two nations will recognize a cultural continuity that cuts across the political boundary, significant social and cultural discontinuities are also apparent. These are often ignored. The differing political structures that separate these two nations have major economic and social consequences for their citizenry. The two countries shape the lives of their inhabitants in distinctive ways. The economic systems of Mexico and the United States are not the same; Mexico's political economy provides its citizens with a lower standard of living than does that of the United States. The discontinuities are even more clearly pronounced because of the fact that in each case, the state controls the educational system. The school system, in turn, plays a major role in shaping the world view of the societies' inhabitants. To speak about cultural continuity without recognizing the discontinuities is to brush aside the importance of nationalism in the everyday life of the people in these two nations. The point is that Mexican Americans do not gain their social identity from Mexico but from their status as citizens of the United States.

The respondents in this study were typically second- to fourth-generation Mexican Americans. Almost all of those who visit Mexico do so as tourists. Although they are aware that their cultural roots have historically been grounded to a considerable degree in Mexican culture, they conceive of themselves as different from Mexicans, and they gain their national social identity, not from Mexico, but from being members of U.S. society (cf. Keefe and Padilla 1987). They recognize significant social and economic differences between themselves and Mexicans.

Overall, then, Mexican Americans share a culture that is neither Mexican national nor Anglo in character. As was suggested above, the Mexican American group includes significant social and cultural variations by region and social class. Moreover, the fact that Mexican Americans in the United States have over the decades been incorporating into their midst various waves of immigration from Mexico has reinforced the distinctiveness of Mexican American culture; this has not, however, made it similar to the culture of Mexico. Instead, Mexican nationals who immigrate to the United States typically settle in Mexican American neighborhoods and acquire many of the cultural patterns of Mexican Americans, if for no other reason than to avoid detection by the U.S. Immigration and Naturalization Service. Then, too, we must recognize that these waves of immigration have contributed to generational and class differences among Mexican Americans that have heightened the social diversity that exists within this ethnic group.

## Mexican Americans and U.S. Society

I have emphasized that Mexican Americans should not be confused with Mexican nationals. Mexican Americans are an ethnic minority group within the United States. But they have been excluded from full participation in activities that the majority sector takes for granted. Nevertheless, while they are set apart and discriminated against in many sectors of society, they are also influenced, in greater or lesser degree, by the many social and cultural changes that are taking place in the broader society, even on a global scale.

A major modification characterizing U.S. society in recent decades relates to the family. Blumstein and Schwartz (1983:25) state that "the American family has changed more in the last thirty years than in the previous two hundred and fifty. This is not an exaggeration." They further contend that "families are in a significant state of flux, and the uncertainty reverberates throughout society" (1983:35).

Even if one does not fully accept Blumstein and Schwartz's generalization, it is quite apparent that family life has been greatly altered. But we should also recognize that these sociologists studied primarily the majority sector and did not take into account minority-group families such as the Mexican American. Certainly the Mexican American family has also been undergoing fundamental revision. It too has been affected by and has been responding to the major upheavals that have occurred in the United States since World War II.

One of the basic assumptions underlying my analysis is that both the families described by Blumstein and Schwartz and the families I discuss herein have been responding to basic social forces within the society at large. Mexican Americans are being affected by fundamental revisions in the organizational structure as well as by shifts in cultural values. In turn, these changes seem to have brought about significant modifications in the social-psychological characteristics of persons in the United States.

By way of background, I outline some of these social and cultural forces that bear directly or indirectly on the manner in which the family has been restructured in recent decades (Goode 1970; Popenoe 1988). Increased urbanization, industrialization (including scientific and technological change), and bureaucratization have deeply affected the society and its members. Mexican Americans have not escaped these effects, for by 1980 more than four out of five Mexican Americans resided in metropolitan areas (Bean and Tienda 1987:86). The rural image of Mexican Americans is a false one. If we take the city proper, San Antonio has a larger percentage of Mexican Americans than of Anglos, and a large segment of the Los Angeles population is Mexican American.

Interwoven with the pattern of industrialization and urbanization has been the growth of large-scale bureaucratic organizations in both the public and private sectors. These have fostered the routinization and segmentation of urban social life and that, too, has affected everyday family life. Along with this has been the growth of an economy based on services rather than manufacturing. Consequently, a number of middle-class Mexican Americans have experienced upward mobility by working, for instance, for federal and other governmental agencies. This structural realignment (and I cannot sort out the causal relations herein) has included the movement of women into the labor force in ever increasing numbers. Sociologists take it for granted that this "subtle revolution" (Smith 1979) has had an impact on family life in diverse ways. All the aforementioned changes are, in turn, linked with the rapid expansion of the educational sector in the United States during recent decades. The percentage of persons who are attending colleges and universities is continuing to increase in U.S. society as a whole.

What we must recognize and emphasize is that these broader structural changes have affected different social classes — as well as different minority groups — in varying ways. For example, Mexican American women have increasingly been part of the urban labor force, but they are heavily concentrated in low-paying occupations. Also, Mexican Americans have not profited, relative to members of the majority sector, from the expansion of the higher educational system in the United States. They not only experience a heavy dropout rate on the primary and secondary grade levels but they are underrepresented among college graduates (although the absolute numbers of college-educated persons has been increasing).

But it is not just that the basic structural changes have affected family life. A variety of shifts in cultural values have had their impact, although sociologists have not traced out this pattern in any systematic way. Alterations in the value system include the rise of a "new individualism" that has been documented by a variety of sociologists (Turner 1976; Zurcher 1977). In recent decades persons have turned inward and made themselves the primary focus of their attention and concern. Thus Lasch (1978) speaks of the emergence of a narcissistic culture. Closely related to this phenomenon is a greater openness regarding sexual and other private spheres of activity.

Similarly, religious beliefs and values differ from those in the past. Although the influence of the moral majority should not be underestimated, it is also true that many sectors of the broader society are somewhat less committed to formal religion today than in the past (Glenn 1987).

Still another aspect of the cultural value system merits attention. The period since World War II has seen a greater stress on equality for minorities and women, although a backlash against this value orientation has also been evident in recent political campaigns and in the negative attitudes toward minorities on certain college campuses in the 1980s. Nevertheless, the civil rights movement, with its emphasis on equality, has opened up political participation to ethnic minority groups, including Mexican Americans (Montejano 1987). And the struggles of women for greater equality have affected the family structure and its central dynamics in a variety of ways.

But the question "Just what do these changes mean for Mexican Americans?" must be addressed. I began this section by referring to Blumstein and Schwartz's generalization about the rapidity of change in the family during recent decades. And I have indicated that this has not occurred in isolation; it is associated with fundamental revisions in the organizational structure and cultural values in the United States. At the same time, these changes do not affect all aspects of the society in a similar manner. The broader societal upheavals have had a very different impact on ethnic minority groups such as Mexican Americans than on the majority sector, especially the Anglo middle class. We must not ignore the exclusion of Mexican Americans from full participation in various spheres of societal activity. But even within the Mexican American group, significant differences exist among classes. Thus, if sociologists are to understand family life in the United States, they must not only study patterns on a societal scale but must also pay attention to how minority-group families have been affected by these global patterns in recent decades.

A recurrent theme in this book is that Mexican Americans are not emulating the majority society (or Anglos). The two groups are responding to basic revisions in the social order in different ways. After all, they occupy very different positions in the social structure. In the concluding section I draw on a variety of evidence from my research findings that supports the view that changes in family life are occurring not because Mexican Americans are striving to be like Anglos but because they are responding to basic changes in the broader social and cultural environment.

## The Research Process

In this section I describe the setting for my research and briefly discuss the data on which I have relied for this study. (The pertinent details are provided in the Appendix.)

The main body of this work is based on research conducted in Austin and Corpus Christi, Texas. In 1980 Austin had a population of 345,109 with 17 percent being identified as "Mexican, Mexican American, Chicano" (U.S. Bureau of the Census 1983a); about 44 percent of Corpus Christi's population of 231,999 belonged to this ethnic group (U.S. Bureau of the Census 1983b).[9] During a period of over two years (1981-83), excluding summers, I conducted in-depth interviews and participant observation in Austin. I carried out in-depth interviews with twenty-two couples in the working class and twenty-one in the business/professional group. (I use the terms *business/professional* and *professional* interchangeably.) Two main criteria were used to distinguish the professional from the working-class group: education and occupation. In addition, I narrowed the focus of my research by interviewing couples in the age group 25-50.

A better understanding of the persons I interviewed can be gained if I take note of their occupations. Within the professional class, the men I interviewed included government administrators, teachers, members of the medical community, and a lawyer. The women included teachers, government administrators, a speech therapist, and a nurse. In contrast, the working-class men held such occupations as barber, mechanic, laborer on a work crew, and electrician; the women functioned in such occupational positions as secretary, clerk, babysitter, and cashier.

Typically the in-depth interviews were conducted for three or four hours. I used an interview guide and thus asked certain basic questions of each respondent. Still, the emphasis throughout has been on the collection of qualitative data. In addition to the in-depth interviews I carried out participant observation in a variety of social settings (Lofland and Lofland 1984). Through this process I was able to collect information on a number of couples who were not part of the initial formal interviews.

The research in Corpus Christi was intended as a means of checking, as well as elaborating on, my findings in Austin. The Corpus Christi fieldwork was conducted during the academic years 1985-86 and 1986-87, and I engaged in full-time research activities during the summers of 1985 and 1986. I interviewed sixteen couples in the working class and a similar number in the professional group. Here again, I collected a significant amount of data through intensive participant observation. Through this process I was able to compare what people said with what they actually did (Deutscher 1973).

In addition to the research in Austin and Corpus Christi, I collected supplemental data on family life in the Kingsville area of South Texas and in a small community south of San Antonio, Texas, during the summers of 1979 through 1983, as well as during shorter periods of time when I visited the Kingsville region.[10] This research has been especially pertinent to my effort to reconstruct traditional life-cycle rituals and their related family forms. Moreover, through informal field observation (Zurcher 1983) I have been able to interact intensively with Mexican American families who are more economically disadvantaged than those I studied in Austin and Corpus Christi. The data on poor families have provided me with a basis for making certain comparative interpretations throughout the book.

Although my fieldwork is quite extensive, I do not claim that the persons I studied are representative of all Mexican Americans in the United States. I suggested earlier that this minority group is much more varied than is often depicted in the literature. Still, this research in Texas takes on special significance on several counts. For one thing, two of the major ethnographic accounts — those by Madsen and by Rubel — which have served as the basis for many sociological generalizations about the traditional Mexican American family, were conducted in small communities in Texas. Thus I am focusing on the same region that certain social scientists have studied with regard to family patterns among Mexican Americans. Also, I have relied on more than one community for my data; thus there is reason to believe that the patterns described, while they may not hold for all Mexican Americans, are nonetheless generalizable beyond the confines of the particular settings I have examined. Indeed, the patterns that I have delineated are applicable to a sizable sector of the Mexican American community.

## Specific Objectives

I am concerned with describing interrelated aspects of family life among Mexican Americans. First, I attempt to reconstruct the basic contours of the traditional family patterns. Second, I examine changes in the extended family system. Third, I analyze women's and men's redefinition of their traditional roles and study the emerging power relationships within the conjugal or nuclear setting. Although the number of never-married, widowed, and divorced persons (many of whom have children) is increasing (Frisbie and Kelly 1985), my focus is on married couples. To be sure, I interacted with a variety of unmarried persons, both men and women, in the course of my field research, but I have not included data on them herein. Instead, my attention is directed to married couples and the extended family system.

The literature on the Mexican American family makes frequent reference to the traditional family. Attention is also given to the extended family and power relationships between husbands and wives, but no one has sought to discuss these in any systematic way. I have specifically used life-cycle rituals—those relating to birth, marriage, and death—[11] as a point of departure for describing traditional family arrangements. I have collected data for the era of the 1920s through the 1950s from persons in their 60s, 70s, and 80s who still live in communities and small towns in South Texas. By studying life-cycle rituals, we can set the extended and conjugal family within a broader community context and examine how family life has been integrated into the religious fabric of Mexican American culture. Knowledge about traditional role expectations is essential. When social scientists analyze alterations in family patterns, the question immediately arises: What is the standard against which we are contrasting the current social arrangements? A number of unproductive debates among social scientists have resulted from the fact that different baselines are used to contrast current social patterns with those in the past. Often social scientists talk past one another and fail to treat the same issue. For example, it would be possible to contrast the present-day Mexican American family with folk societies, pre-industrial civilized societies, and so forth. I am taking the traditional family patterns of some decades ago as my point of departure.

This argument suggests still another reason for placing the current ethnographic data about family life within the context of tradition. There is a body of theory and research, at least with regard to societies as a whole, that demonstrates that persons do not give up all aspects of tradition when change occurs. Change is not linear in nature. The "old" and the "new" are interpreted and shaped as human beings interact with one another in complex ways. We must come to realize that although traditional patterns have undergone revision, they still play a role in the everyday life of people on the contemporary urban scene (cf. Geertz, 1973).

The second major objective of this research is to study how the extended family is being restructured. When discussing Mexican American family life, social scientists have emphasized that *la familia* — the extended family — is a central aspect of the culture (they often forget that it is also central to most other cultural groups as well). Nevertheless, we know little about how *la familia* has undergone basic revisions over time. Sena-Rivera (1979) and Keefe and Padilla (1987) contend, on the basis of their research, that the extended family is still an integral part of Mexican American life, while other scholars see a breakdown in this structure. By focusing on contemporary life-cycle rituals — those relating to birth, marriage, and death — we are able to trace some basic revisions that have occurred in the extended family. More specifically, the compadrazgo ritual as it is associated with the birth of a child (discussed in Chapter 2) is frequently cited as having undergone change in urban areas (Grebler et al. 1970). No one, however, has carried out research detailing just how this ritual has been modified. The same can be said of weddings and funerals.

The changes with respect to funerals take on special significance. During the course of this research it became evident why Durkheim (1915) placed major emphasis on rituals associated with death, for death involves a major rupture in social relations and highlights certain aspects of life for the living. The social activities surrounding death bring to the fore features of the social interaction (or lack thereof) by family members that are unlikely to be grasped through other means. This strong claim is supported by the data I have collected.

A by-product of this research is that through studying life-cycle rituals I have acquired an understanding of certain aspects of the emerging religious beliefs and practices among Mexican Americans. We have few empirical studies on this facet of Mexican American life. Yet religion has been an integral feature of life-cycle rituals, especially funerals, and thus we must give it considerable attention. In a more general sense, by examining the new meanings that persons are attaching to the new ritual patterns, we come to understand the emerging nature of religious life and how this is related to family life among Mexican Americans.[12]

A third major objective with respect to the Mexican American family is to understand role making and decision making by husbands and wives. Ultimately I am intent on understanding the current power relationships between men and women in the conjugal setting.

In the current literature on the Mexican American family two divergent views of the family are set forth. There is the traditional view of husbands as authoritarian or dominant; they are viewed as having almost absolute control over their wives and daughters. This conception of family life can be traced to the ethnographic accounts of Madsen, Rubel, and others, discussed above.

More recent findings have led some social scientists to conclude that Mexican American husband-wife relationships are egalitarian in nature. Building on the widely cited work on decision making by Blood and Wolfe (1960), a number of researchers—Cromwell and Cromwell (1978), Hawkes and Taylor (1975), and Ybarra (1977, 1982)—have arrived at this conclusion. Ybarra (1982:177) reports that her study also "supported the findings of recent empirical studies conducted in different regions of the country which concluded that egalitarianism is the predominant conjugal role arrangement in Chicano families." Nonetheless, this research tradition, as we later see, is severely limited by its reliance upon survey data.

Although Zavella (1987) has recently questioned the findings regarding egalitarianism in the Mexican American family, she and others have not carried out research focused directly on the problem of changing power relationships in the conjugal family. Instead, they have typically gathered data only on the women's point of view. I have sought to collect information, through in-depth interviews and participant observation, from the perspective of both husbands and wives. In addition, it is through understanding role making that we come to comprehend more fully the nature of decision making between married couples. Most of the literature on decision making has taken a very static view of what actually is a complex social process. Although I do not claim to deal with all the questions in this large body of literature, I attempt to show how divergent findings about social power in the conjugal family have arisen and how we might more effectively understand present-day relationships between husbands and wives.

In studying role making and decision making within the conjugal family we must also understand that these processes do not operate independently of the broader community and organizational setting. The resistance to role making by Mexican American women on the part of husbands and community organizations in the public sphere places these women in a difficult situation as they strive to deal with being "twice a minority." Because it is the women, not the men, who typically initiate role making within the family setting, I give special attention to role making by married women who experience negative reactions from others because of their gender and ethnicity.

The preceding comments bring to the fore a fourth major objective of this book: an effort to understand the role of Mexican American women as "twice a minority." Minority women have been much neglected in research on gender roles and family life in the United States (Shapiro 1986). The research I have conducted brings new data on the position of Mexican American women vis-à-vis women in the privileged majority.

## General Objectives

The specific objectives outlined above are supported by rather extensive qualitative data on the nature of the traditional Mexican American family as well as fundamental revisions in the extended and conjugal family during recent decades. I also have a more ambitious, and more general, objective in mind. I indicate how symbolic interactionism must be modified and extended so as to place ethnographic data on the daily activities of family life within a broader social setting. Earlier in this chapter, I indicated that we must view the contemporary Mexican American family in the context of social and cultural change in the broader society. This is in keeping with Marcus and Fischer's (1986) contention that modern ethnographers must interpret their data on the micro level within a more macro context. In the process I attempt to contribute to the sociology of the family in a fundamental sense.

In this section I sketch out only some features of the theoretical framework that I am utilizing in this study; then I elaborate on specific issues in the process of analyzing the data that I have collected. The general orientation of symbolic interactionists provides us with an understanding of how people in everyday life interpret the ongoing social processes that emerge as a result of interaction among persons. This framework has its foundations in the work of George Herbert Mead (1934) and his primary sociological interpretator, Herbert Blumer (1969). Some of its essential features may appear rather elemental, but its principles diverge sharply from, for example, exchange theory, which has been so widely employed in recent decades for interpreting family life.

From the perspective of symbolic interactionism (Blumer 1969), persons interact toward "things" — humans as well as objects — in terms of the meanings these have for them. In turn, these meanings are not static but emerge out of people's interaction with others. Moreover, it is in the process of human interaction that human beings come to interpret and reinterpret both objects and persons. In a general sense, symbolic interactionism stresses that the "self" and "mind" and "needs" are social in nature and do not have a fixed existence within human beings. Unlike some exchange theorists, who emphasize a biopsychological conception of human beings as intrinsically unchangeable and view persons as acting in terms of "self-interest," a symbolic interactionists' conception of human beings stresses that the nature of human nature is quite malleable and that persons respond to situations in a variety of ways.

My use of a symbolic interaction framework makes extensive use of the concept of social role. We need not consider herein all the debates sociologists and social psychologists have had with one another about the meaning and use of this concept (Biddle 1986). Whatever the differences among social scientists regarding the concept of social role, it nonetheless remains useful for bridging the gap between individuals on the one hand and the broader society on the other. The concept "social role" provides us with an understanding of the activities of husbands, wives, and other members of the kinship system.

Symbolic interactionists have emphasized that human beings learn their roles and carry them out by taking the roles of others. Through role taking, persons develop a conception of the self and sustain stability in their relationships with others. In studying change, however, we must move beyond the idea of role taking and recognize the significance of role making. Ralph Turner (1962) introduced the concept of role making into sociology. Although his work has been widely cited, his conceptual innovation has seldom been employed in the analysis of research data. It is ironic that Turner (1970), in his *Family Interaction*, which is one of the few major works systematically to employ symbolic interaction in interpreting contemporary family life, did not utilize the conceptual scheme he had constructed some years earlier.

The ideas associated with role making serve as a guiding framework for analyzing changing patterns in the Mexican American family. But to make effective use of the role-making framework we must modify symbolic interactionism in several ways. We must incorporate such concepts as "tradition," "social memory," the "social mind" and "contradictions" into our conceptual framework in order to interpret role making by Mexican American men and women.

Symbolic interactionists, because of their focus on contemporary urban patterns, have typically given little or no attention to "tradition," for this notion suggests the need to incorporate a historical perspective into one's analysis. Nevertheless, if we are to examine traditional Mexican American family patterns, which become the baseline for interpreting the changes that are occurring, we must of necessity incorporate a historical dimension into our analysis. But the meaning of tradition for persons can be grasped only if we acknowledge that people may or may not share a "social memory" of past social arrangements. We must be attentive to how they interpret tradition in terms of their current social situation. I argue that this kind of role-making process cannot be examined without incorporating the "social mind."

Symbolic interactionists have stressed the "social self" and lent scant attention to the "social mind." But, it is difficult to conceive of the self as having a memory. It is the social mind, with its capacity to reflect back on itself and store memory of past experiences, that becomes an important means for grasping the process of role making by human agents (Smith 1982; Vaughan and Sjoberg 1984; Collins 1989). It is through reflectivity that human agents may purposely reshape their identity and their roles.

To understand contemporary role-making patterns it is also necessary that this process be viewed within the context of complex organizational and community settings (McCall and Simmons 1982). With respect to understanding role making by Mexican Americans, especially women, we quickly perceive that role making can be restricted in significant ways by the larger social context. The process of discrimination within the broader community has rather direct effects on role-making patterns within the familial context. This is one of the theoretical themes that has emerged from my research.

Finally, we must recognize that as a result of social change, "contradictory role expectations" arise within both the family and the community setting. There is a tendency within sociology to rely too heavily on the strain toward consistency as a principle for understanding social relationships. My own research indicates that many of the persons I studied have learned to live with what Zurcher (1986b) calls a "cognitive dialectic." If this were not so, they would be unable to meet the contradictory expectations that they encounter and, in the face of an onslaught to the self, to maintain a sense of self worth. This holds especially for women who must interact with members of the broader community as "twice a minority."

In sum, I employ symbolic interactionism as a general framework for understanding the field data. But, I have greatly modified this orientation as it has typically been employed so as more realistically to interpret the field research findings that I have collected on changing family patterns among Mexican Americans. In succeeding chapters I elaborate upon the aforementioned theoretical issues as these become relevant for making sense of the data and then in the concluding chapter I treat more fully the implications of my conceptual innovations for symbolic interactionism.

## Analysis of the Data and Presentation of the Findings

Although I carried out in-depth interviews, my focus was on the collection of qualitative data. Moreover, as the project progressed, data gathered through participant observation became increasingly important for interpreting the data from the interviews. One of the perennial problems facing qualitative researchers is how to present their findings. Some research reports leave the impression that the patterns described hold for all the persons studied. In many works (e.g., Rubin 1976; Stack 1974) the reader is hard pressed to discern any variation on the routine set of role expectations.

Although it is essential for social scientists to generalize from their findings, it should be recognized that variability regarding social relations always exists, and it tends to be heightened during periods of rapid social and cultural change. Thus, attention needs to be devoted not only to the similarities but also to some of the diversities in the empirical world.

In analyzing the data on the Mexican American family I focus on two major kinds of patterns.[13] One involves situations in which only modest variations exist in present-day social arrangements. Yet, even here, some attention to differences may be in order. In the second instance there is considerable diversity regarding familial activities, and no dominant pattern has yet emerged. To understand the contemporary Mexican American family we must consider those situations involving a great deal of variability.

In order to provide the necessary background for understanding present-day patterns I first analyze the traditional family arrangements as they have been expressed through life-cycle rituals within the community setting (see Chapter 2). This chapter also provides background data on gender roles, as well as religious beliefs in the traditional Mexican American culture. In Chapters 3 and 4 I consider life-cycle rituals in the contemporary urban setting, first in the working class and then in the business and professional class. These chapters, in particular, emphasize the restructuring of extended family arrangements that has taken place in recent decades. During this period of change, certain traditions have been modified and sustained, while others are disappearing.

Chapter 5 considers role making and decision making in the conjugal family in the working class; this is followed by Chapter 6, which discusses these patterns in the professional/business class. I emphasize that we cannot understand decision-making patterns without first recognizing how men and women are reshaping their traditional roles. The special attention given to role making by women who are "twice a minority" is a distinctive contribution of the present work.

In the last chapter I examine in considerable detail the theoretical implications of changes in the Mexican American family. And I give special attention to how these changes differ from those in the majority sector of the society. We cannot understand the family patterns of minority groups unless we place them within the context of the majority sector. Yet my data point to the fact that in interpreting the family life of Mexican Americans it cannot be assumed that these persons are attempting to emulate and become like the majority. Both the majority and minority are responding to broader social and cultural forces in the society, but they are doing so in rather divergent ways.

# Notes

1. Among the many studies that depend on surveys (including those by the U.S. Census Bureau) for data on selected aspects of Mexican American family patterns are Bean and Tienda (1987), Bean and Swicegood (1985), and Frisbie, Bean, and Eberstein (1978). Moreover, most of the research on intermarriage—such as that by Murguia (1982)—has utilized official marriage records.

2. Many of the criticisms by social scientists regarding the early research on Mexican American family life have been primarily theoretical in nature and have not been grounded in empirical research. For example, the writings by Montiel (1970), Staples and Mirandé (1980), and Mirandé (1985) have been widely cited but are not based on original research materials. Baca Zinn (1975, 1976, 1980, 1982) has been one of the few scholars in the 1970s to anchor critical comments in original field research.

Also, much of the commentary on Mexican American women (or Chicanas) has been based not on field research in contemporary urban settings but on critical theoretical reflections. For an informative summary of this research, see Baca Zinn (1984). Among the important works to be consulted are Griswold del Castillo (1984), De Leon (1983), and Mirandé and Enríquez (1979). More recent works by Zavella (1987) and Ruiz (1987) have been grounded in careful field or historical research.

3. Horowitz (1983), in her study of an inner-city Chicano community in Chicago, describes Mexican American women as subordinate to men and perceives of a daughter as a "virgin" and a married woman solely as a "mother." She writes "Women must be either wives, sisters, or mothers to men" (p. 70). Also, "a young woman's identity is linked not only to her sexuality but to her feminine behavior—forgiving, submissive, and not aggressive" (p. 132). Horowitz describes men as dominant. For example, "A son, like any man, is expected to be independent and dominant in any social relationship with women" (p. 63). On theoretical as well as empirical grounds these generalizations must be questioned.

It should be noted that a number of sociologists have accepted Horowitz's generalizations in an uncritical manner (e.g., Hutter 1988).

4. I find the conceptual distinction between the "private" and the "public" spheres to be a useful one for clarifying certain empirical aspects of family life, especially with respect to Mexican American women. Nonetheless, one should be aware of the controversy regarding this analytical perspective. See, e.g., Nicholson 1986.

5. Several case studies by well-known anthropologists have basically left women out of their research reports. One is the description of a Japanese village by Embree (1939). For an informative account of how women of the village were generally ignored in this research, see Smith and Wiswell (1982). Also, Weiner (1976) has sought to correct the writings of the famous anthropologist Malinowski, who tended to neglect the important role of women in his work on the Trobriand Islanders.

6. A considerable number of scholars have attempted to link Mexican Americans with the culture of Mexico and even the Aztec heritage (Mirandé and Enríquez 1979). Although the Mexican American culture is grounded upon many of the cultural traditions of Mexico, I have serious reservations about interpreting the life experiences of present-day Mexican Americans in these terms.

It must be emphasized that the culture of Mexico is itself a complex amalgam of a number of Indian and Spanish traditions. Although Mexican American culture has built on this heritage, scholars who stress the Mexican past often fail to highlight the distinctive aspects of Mexican American culture within the United States.

7. I typically employ the term Mexican American in this study. One reason is that the persons whom I studied typically identified themselves as Mexican Americans and not as Chicanos. And I have attempted to remain faithful to the perspective of those who cooperated

with me in this research effort. Nevertheless, I use the terms Mexican Americans and Chicanos interchangeably, with Chicanos referring to Mexican American men or to both males and females and Chicanas referring to Mexican American women.

8. When attempting to define Mexican Americans, we must also note that certain Mexican American scholars have been influenced by a movement that has sought to establish cultural bonds between Mexico and Mexican Americans and in the process to construct a transnational Mexicanism. One of the intellectual leaders of this movement has been the prominent Mexican sociologist Jorge Bustamante.

9. The problems associated with identifying Mexican Americans in the 1980 census are in part discussed by Tienda and Ortiz (1986).

10. Included in the Kingsville region are such communities as Falfurrias and Alice. In 1980 Kingsville had a population of 28,808; over half were of "Mexican origin." Falfurrias had a population of 6,145, which was overwhelmingly of "Mexican origin" (U. S. Bureau of the Census 1983c).

11. I have not stressed the quinceañera (fifteenth birthday celebration) ritual, but I did acquire some data on this life-cycle ritual.

12. The interrelationships of religion and family life are examined in various essays in D'Antonio and Aldous (1983). Some of the theoretical issues raised are relevant to research on Mexican American family life.

13. I have sought to avoid one of the problems that plagues Rubel's (1966) analysis of Mexican American culture. At times he takes patterns that reflect exaggerations of everyday life and gives the reader the impression that these are typical. For example, in his discussion of "machismo" he illustrates the pattern by noting how one father slapped his daughter. While this incident may have occurred, my own interviews with Mexican Americans over 60 years of age in the Kingsville region provide no justification for believing that the slapping of daughters was a typical response by fathers who reacted negatively to actions they did not approve of.

Chapter **2** **TRADITIONAL LIFE-CYCLE RITUALS AMONG MEXICAN AMERICANS IN TEXAS**

Contemporary American sociologists have given little attention to examining the interrelationships between life-cycle rituals and family life. It is true that Caplow and his colleagues (1982) discussed the place of rituals such as Thanksgiving and Christmas in the lives of families in Middletown. Nevertheless, ceremonial activities surrounding birth, marriage, and death receive scant attention in most monographs or textbooks on the family.[1]

Several factors seem to account for this neglect of life-cycle rituals. One is that many specialists on the family have tended to overlook the rich intellectual tradition of scholars such as van Gennep (1960), Durkheim (1915), and Eliade (1957). For Durkheim and Eliade, in particular, the analysis of rituals was a means for understanding the role of religion in daily life. Their focus, however, was not on the family. As a result, the concept of ritual often connotes the study of religion, not the family or the interrelationships between religious beliefs and familial ties. Another possible reason for the neglect of life-cycle rituals is that these have been minimized in most sectors of U.S. society. For instance, coping with a death in the family has become for many persons a "private" rather than a "public" matter, and the ceremonial activities relating to death have consequently been greatly reduced.

Many works on Mexican American culture make some mention of "compadrazgo" (as it is associated with infant baptism), and they often refer to certain traditional patterns of mourning. But no one has drawn a relatively coherent picture of life-cycle rituals and family life in the Mexican American culture.

Whatever the reasons for the neglect of study of the relationships between life-cycle rituals and family activities, research on the Mexican American family affords us a unique opportunity to demonstrate the interconnection between the past and the present.

### The Social Significance of Life-cycle Rituals

Van Gennep (1960) was one of the first social scientists to recognize that life-cycle rituals mark important transition points in the life of individuals — principally, when they are born, when they get married, and when they die. Durkheim (1915), focusing specifically on ceremonial activities surrounding death, emphasized the major role these play in helping persons adjust to major ruptures in their lives.

Fried and Fried (1980), who have presented a useful survey of life-cycle rituals and the forms they take in different cultures, have observed: "Every known human society, simple or complex, whatever its economic or political structure, provides for ritually divided phases of life" (p. 14). Life-cycle rituals thus appear to be a human universal, although their specific cultural content may vary considerably across cultures.

The social significance of these rituals rests on the fact that they highlight points of social transition for human beings in the life cycle. During these rituals, deep-seated human emotions are shaped through human interaction. Ceremonies marking birth and marriage are meant to express joy and celebration. Those marking death connote sadness and grief.

Moreover, life-cycle ceremonies make it known to the participants, as well as the broader social order, that major shifts in role expectations are in order. As a result of the birth of a child, husband and wife assume new obligations, and as a result of a death, a spouse becomes widowed. The affected persons must accept a new definition of themselves not only within the family but also within the community.

As in many traditional cultures, the life-cycle rituals of Mexican American families have linked the conjugal family to the broader extended family and to friendship circles within the community. More specifically, these rituals bring to the fore role expectations by men and women in both the extended and conjugal family systems. In turn, the interaction patterns that have been an integral feature of these rituals have reinforced and been reinforced by the religious belief system. Thus the traditional life-cycle rituals cannot be understood apart from the religious commitments of the participants.

## The Nature of Tradition among Mexican Americans

Up to this point I have taken the relationship between rituals and tradition for granted. But, a number of issues, both theoretical and empirical, require clarification if we are to relate the traditional life-cycle rituals among Mexican Americans not only to traditional family arrangements but to the current patterns as well.

### Rituals, Tradition, and Sacred Time

Symbolic interactionists have focused heavily on the fluid nature of modern urban life and have overlooked the fact that tradition[2] has long played a vital role in human interaction. Eliade (1957), perhaps more than any scholar, has captured the meaning of rituals in the maintenance of tradition. In analyzing ritual activities he distinguished between those associated with "sacred time" and those associated with "secular time." Time is not some fixed external reality; instead, it is a social and cultural construct. Nowhere is this more apparent than in rituals, particularly those that reinforce the "sacred religious tradition." Eliade recognized that through sacred rituals, people attempt to arrest time. For example, in the celebration of the Lord's Supper, the participants seek to reenact the event, even to the point of "duplicating" patterns as they are believed to have been. In practice, we know that rituals change over time. Still, the participants engaged in "sacred rituals" are seeking to preserve the past. Through their social (or "collective") memory, the participants attempt to recapture or recreate the activities of their forefathers. Memory is possible because human beings have a "social mind" (with the capacity for reflection and memory) and not just a "social self." Yet, in this type of social setting there are "eternal truths" that are not subject to relativistic interpretations.

Symbolic interactionists such as Blumer (1969), as well as Goffman (1959), who adheres to a dramaturgical orientation, have stressed the role of creativity and fluidity in human life. The actors they describe are oriented to the present and are disinterested in a social world that is limited by a commitment to sacred time. Thus, Goffman's (1967) analysis of ritual concerns social interaction of a highly stylized sort that involves no effort by human agents to recapture sacred time, or a sacred tradition more generally (cf. Deegan in press).

Yet we should remember that although human interaction is always processual in nature, many Mexican Americans just a few decades ago lived in a social setting in which role expectations were relatively fixed and the sacred tradition continued relatively intact. This does not mean that change did not occur. People did reflect on their interactions with others, but they did so within far narrower confines than is the case today. The nature of the role expectations, as well as the "resources" of family members, did not permit the range of creative action that is part of everyday life today in at least the privileged sectors of U.S. society.

### Tradition among Mexican Americans

Advantages as well as disadvantages accrue from the use of Central and, especially, South Texas as a base for reconstructing traditional Mexican American family life. In the introduction, I discussed briefly the emergence of a Mexican American culture that differs from that of Mexico and the dominant Anglo society.

Several other aspects of the historical setting, not mentioned previously, seem relevant here. Those Mexicans who became U.S. citizens in the mid-nineteenth century had settled on the northern frontier of Mexico, a region that differed considerably from the interior (which itself is varied and complex). On the frontier, the formal structure of the Catholic church was not so elaborate and its influence on the people not so great as in the interior (Weber 1981); this meant that folk traditions, especially in the realm of religion, played a prominent role in the frontier culture.

The development of a Mexican American culture that differed appreciably from the culture of Mexico and the majority Anglo society was also fostered by the virtual exclusion of Mexican Americans from the economic and social systems of mainstream U.S. society. On the one hand, Mexican Americans were designated as U.S. citizens; on the other hand, they were relegated to a second-class status in their new country. A number of prominent Texas historians of the past downgraded Mexican Americans and failed to recognize their contributions to the shaping of the cultural landscape of the Southwest. Only in recent years have younger groups of historians been seeking to correct the record (Jackson 1986; Chavez 1984). For example, Jackson has pointed up that vital aspects of the ranching and cowboy culture of the Southwest owe their origins to traditions carried over from Mexico.

The educated elite in Mexico had little interest in the frontier and therefore neglected to record the lives of its inhabitants. So, too, Anglo historians and even travelers did little to document the early life of Mexican Americans. Although it has been a slow process, a historical record of Mexican Americans is now accumulating. In a sense, though, Mexican Americans have been, in Wolf's (1982) terminology, "a people without history."

These historical patterns are important as a backdrop for our examination of traditional life-cycle rituals within the Mexican American culture. Perhaps future historians will piece together data that will lead to a better understanding of life in the present century and earlier. But even Paredes (1958), who perhaps more than anyone else has captured the culture of Mexican Americans in Texas, provides only sketchy patterns about family life in his research on the Mexican American culture at the beginning of this century (cf. Foley et al. 1988:52-62).[3]

As a result, I have had to reconstruct traditions through other means. I have relied heavily on strategic respondents. Most of these persons lived in the Kingsville region and were over 60 years of age; a number were in their 70s and 80s. Thus, they could recall patterns and in some instances remember what their parents and other relatives told them about specific rituals. Some of the respondents in Austin and Corpus Christi who were in their 40s also had knowledge or a keen social memory of the traditional life-cycle rituals and family patterns that I describe in this study. And I have talked with other selected persons from different parts of Texas about these rituals.

My generalizations are typically applicable to the 1930s through the 1950s, although the recollections of a few respondents go back to the 1920s. Moreover, I have also relied on published accounts. Some of the descriptive data by Madsen (1964) and Rubel (1966), for example, are relevant here.

## The Religious Context

Inasmuch as religion permeated the lives of Mexican Americans until a few decades ago, I elaborate further on the function of religion as a basis for understanding life-cycle rituals. These have been especially meaningful for persons in social orders that stress the sacredness of human existence. All the data we have on Mexican Americans indicate that religion, notably Roman Catholicism, in the past played a compelling role in everyday life. It was not just that people attended church (except on the ranches, or "ranchitos," and in some of the small rural communities of South Texas where churches did not exist) but that their lives were permeated by religion. Within the home, altars and other religious symbols were often prominently displayed. Although the degree of their devoutness varied, people prayed often and interpreted many happenings as evidence of "God's will." For example, fatalistic phrases such as "Está en las manos de Dios" (It's in God's hands) or "Si Dios quiere" (If God wills it) and "Que será será" (Whatever will be, will be) were still heard in many Mexican American neighborhoods of South Texas until rather recently. We must be careful not to stamp Mexican Americans as being particularly fatalistic, however, as Rubel and Madsen and other social scientists have done, for fatalism has characterized all traditional social orders and continues within certain subgroups in modern societies.

We must be mindful that in the past Mexican Americans had to struggle hard to make a living, and when illness or other misfortunes befell them, they were able to exert little control over the situation. Attributing untoward occurrences to God's will or to fate permitted a form of adaptation to difficult life circumstances.

As in most traditional social orders, the women were the primary carriers of the religious belief system. The very nature of the hierarchy of the Roman Catholic church and of its traditional teachings has called for women to be subordinate to men and to serve as devoted daughters, wives, and mothers. Not surprisingly, it is the women who have been the most expressive in the area of religion, for they have done most of the praying and churchgoing. And it is mainly the women who have been expected to instill the religious belief system in their children. Mothers have spent more time with young children than have fathers. Under these circumstances, mothers have played an active role in disciplining their children and socializing them into the cultural belief system of Mexican Americans, including the teachings of the Roman Catholic church as they have understood them. We know that persons lacking formal education have not understood the religious teachings in all their complexities, but they have grasped the central aspects of the doctrine and have sought to pass these on to their children.

In general, then, Mexican American women have played an active role in the home and in the practice of religion. They have cared for the children and carried out a variety of tasks, not just in the household but at times also in the fields. Under these circumstances, they could hardly have been the passive and weak beings that social scientists' stereotypes have made them out to be.

Nonetheless, there have been contradictory definitions of women's roles. On the one hand, wives and daughters have been defined as subordinate to their husbands and fathers, and this has been reinforced by the religious belief system. But they have also been viewed as deceptive and not to be trusted sexually. (What is often not recognized is that women, because of their subordinate position, have often had to act in a deceptive fashion, from the male perspective, in order to sustain some control over their lives.) On the other hand, women, particularly mothers, have been defined as madonna-like.

The aforementioned pattern seems to overlap with an image of women in Mexican American culture that is often mentioned in social science literature. This is the "good/bad woman" image. There is a tendency to classify individual women as belonging to either of two categories: the good woman or the bad woman. Good women are those who are married and stay at home and take care of their husbands and children. These women are deeply devoted to furthering the maintenance of ideal family patterns. In contrast are the bad women, who enter the public sphere and become stereotyped as prostitutes and barmaids. This is the so-called madonna-whore dichotomy.

This contradictory image of women, which is rather typical of traditional cultural settings (and not just among Mexican Americans), has created special problems for social scientists in their interpretation of the role of women in traditional Mexican American families. And these opposing images of women, as we later see, persist in subtle ways and present considerable difficulties for interpreting the role of Mexican American women in the modern urban family and community setting (a point to which we return in later chapters).

### The Birth Ceremony

Here we describe the general patterns of compadrazgo (literally, co-parenthood) associated with infant baptism. Compadrazgo may also apply to some other life-cycle rituals—for example, first communion, confirmation, marriage, and los quince años (the fifteenth-birthday celebration for a girl that has traditionally been celebrated in the Catholic church and involves the practice of selecting ritual sponsors or padrinos).[4] But infant baptism is the basic ritual in which ties of compadrazgo are established between parents and godparents and child and godparents. It is also a typical means of creating what scholars have referred to as a "fictive kinship system."

In the traditional culture expectant parents would select a married couple from among their close friends (or, occasionally, extended family members) to be the child's sponsors at a baptismal ceremony (see e.g., Rubel 1966; Grebler et al. 1970; Valle 1974). Ideally such sponsors—who were called padrino and madrina by the child and compadre and comadre by the parents—should have been married in the Catholic church. An invitation to be a sponsor was considered a special honor that should not be refused.

It was not unusual for the couple to be sponsors for one or more of the child's younger siblings as well. Many Mexican Americans have adhered to the belief that the same padrinos should serve in the baptism of three of their children, for such would "make the sign of the cross" ("hacer la cruz"), a gesture that has symbolic religious meaning in Catholicism (cf. Rubel 1966:81).

The religious meaning of this ritual was anchored in the belief that an infant is born in original sin. Thus the baby must, through baptism, be cleansed of this sin to be received into heaven.

Because of the deeply held religious commitments of Mexican Americans some decades ago, a baby was baptized within three to fifteen weeks after birth. There was a sense of urgency because if an unbaptized child died, his or her soul would go to Limbo (a place where a person would not suffer pain but would be severed from God).

The parents and padrinos, as faithful Catholics, took their religious beliefs seriously. In addition, grandparents would pressure to have their grandchildren baptized as early as possible. They, especially, stressed the significance of the bond established between parents, children, and godparents.

According to the traditional custom, the baptismal sponsors were responsible for purchasing the white christening outfit as well as a cap, a diaper, diaper pins, socks, booties, and so on. The godmother dressed the baby for the occasion. If the sponsors had sufficient means, they presented the baby with a gold ring or a little gold medallion as a keepsake.

The baptismal ceremony was conducted in church on Sunday after the last morning mass or in the afternoon. At the minimum the ceremony included the priest, the child, the child's parents, and the two sponsors, and oftentimes members of the extended family, especially the grandparents. The madrina (or godmother) held the baby during the ceremony as the priest blessed the infant by making the sign of the cross on its forehead and chest with holy water, salt, and oils, and by breathing on its body.

The priest also placed a white cloth over the child's chest while conducting the blessing. In addition, he lit a candle to symbolize religious and moral guidance for the child and to mark the beginning of the child's spiritual life. After the ceremony, the padrinos made a monetary contribution to the church.

Next, a celebration was held at the parents' home. The size of the guest list depended on the size of the family's friendship circle and its economic status. Some families invited only the sponsors; for many others, it was a major social occasion with numerous guests in attendance. Extended family members as well as friends were among those present. The former included grandparents, aunts and uncles, and first cousins. The baptismal ceremony was thereby one means of sustaining ties among extended family members.

Mexican food was served for dinner. It included carne guisada (cubed meat in a tomato sauce) or cabrito guisado (stewed kid goat meat), rice, beans, tortillas, beer, chocolate, and cake. In some areas of Texas, pollo en mole (chicken in mole sauce) or barbecued beef was served. Sometimes only lighter refreshments, such as chocolate or coffee and sweet rolls or wedding cookies (pan de polvo), were offered.

Gender divisions were very much in evidence. In the postbaptismal activities, the socializing pattern consisted of the men talking and drinking outside the house and the women visiting with one another inside the home. The women prepared the food and served it first to the men. They worked hard to take care of the children while preparing and serving food in a situation where they had none of the conveniences of modern urban middle-class life.

It is the postceremonial patterns that are most significant for understanding the functions of compadrazgo. The natural parents and the godparents addressed each other as compadre (co-father) and comadre (co-mother). They treated each other with utmost respect and trust. In essence they deferred to one another and used the formal pronoun *Usted* in direct address instead of the informal *tú*.

A number of social scientists who have examined Mexican American culture have stressed the importance of respect. Although it is revealed in a variety of social settings, it surely is highlighted in the interrelationships between co-parents. Anglo social scientists seem to have been sensitive to the pattern of respect in traditional Mexican American culture. Nevertheless, they often fail to recognize that the role of respect is not unique if seen in a cross-cultural context.

Compadres and comadres visited with each other most frequently in a setting outside the home and came to each other's assistance in time of social and economic need (cf. Clark 1959; Achor 1978). Comadres spent time with each other within their respective homes and during periods of crisis such as illness, and they prepared food as a gesture of concern. Thus compadres and comadres established strong bonds of mutual aid or reciprocity. It was not just the parents who were assisted by the godparents; the former assisted the latter as well.

The relationship between the child and his or her godparents deserves special consideration. The godchild and godparent were called ahijado (or ahijada) and padrino (or madrina), respectively. And they addressed each other by the appropriate terms whenever they met. Thus Rubel (1966:81) observes that "a couple which sponsors a child at its baptismal ceremony thenceforth relates to that child as its padrinos de pila or padrinos de bautismo" (godparents of the baptismal font or of baptism). The ritual parents were seen as accepting the responsibility for taking care of the spiritual and physical needs of the child in the absence of the parents. As the child grew up, the padrino and madrina gave the godchild gifts on special occasions. In the event of the death of the parents, the godparents were expected to rear the child.

Nevertheless, it must be emphasized that the major social bond resulting from the baptismal ceremony is that between parents and godparents. The baptismal ceremony brought these two families into a fictive kinship relationship. True, the child was the focal point of the ritual bond and was frequently referred to in conversation between the co-parents (compadres). And through the years the parents would keep the child informed about the welfare of the godparents.

The creation of fictive kinship arrangements is often commented on because it sets the Mexican American family apart from most groups in the United States. Grebler et al. (1970:354) observed:

> The functional implications of the *compadrazgo* are complex.
> To follow one implication, its persistence may be taken to mean
> that Mexican Americans use a kinship prototype for relation-
> ships that other Americans differentiate from their kin.

The godparenthood pattern among Mexican Americans should, however, not be confused with that in Mexico and other parts of Latin America. According to Wolf and Hansen (1972), the most frequent kind of compadrazgo in Latin America is the vertical form. Vertical compadrazgo is "formed between people, of whom one is wealthier, of higher social standing, and more powerful politically than the other" (1972:132).

Among Mexican Americans, the godparents generally were of equal social standing with the parents. As stressed earlier, the godparent was expected to take care of the physical and spiritual needs of the child in the event that the parents could not perform these essential duties. And reciprocal ties were formed between the parents and the godparents. Both parties were expected to assist each other in time of social or economic need (cf. Clark 1959; Achor 1978).

## The Marriage Ceremony

The next major ceremonial activity in which everyone was expected to participate is the marriage ceremony. To be sure (as noted above), Mexican Americans held a quinceañera rite for young women on their fifteenth birthday, but I have not examined this herein.

I have stressed the commonality of Mexican American patterns with those in traditional social orders — not in terms of content but in terms of form. I have done so in order to emphasize that while Mexican Americans have distinctive patterns that deserve special attention in their own right, we must place them in a comparative perspective.

It was taken for granted that all men and women would marry and have children, and many did so in their teens. This was reinforced by the beliefs of the Catholic church, where marriage and childbearing are considered to be part of God's plan for human beings. Marriage was vital, for homemaking and the bearing and rearing of children were considered the ultimate fulfillment of a woman's life in this world.

As to the specific cultural patterns associated with marriage among Mexican Americans, we can begin a discussion of the role of the portador, or intermediary. Dating, as it has currently evolved, was not acceptable within the traditional Mexican American culture. True, the bride and groom usually had met and known each other through the school, the church, or other community activities, but parents exerted considerable control over their children's (especially their daughter's) choice of a marriage partner. (Among the poor many variations from these ideal expectations were to be found.)

The main function of the portador was to present the young man's marriage proposal to the young woman's parents, especially her father. As in many traditional societies, a go-between permitted the families involved to avoid the possibility of direct rejection and consequent loss of face for all parties involved. To have one's son or daughter perceived as unacceptable as a marriage partner would constitute a serious affront.

Typically, the portador was an older man who was highly respected in the community. In some instances the portador was the young man's baptismal godparent or a member of his extended family, perhaps an uncle. One respondent noted that "someone in my husband's family was a portador. He was good, so a lot of people asked him." Again, variations on this pattern existed. One elderly Mexican American recalled that at times a priest would act an intermediary, sometimes accompanied by another priest. Such a situation would occur if, for example, the young man did not have parents who were living.

The portador's reputation rested on his success in obtaining a positive response from the young woman's parents. And a successful outcome would be known throughout the community, which in turn would enhance his prestige among his peers and in the community as a whole.

The portador first wrote a letter or sent word informally to the young woman's father requesting an appointment for a visitation. In his reply, the father set the date and hour of the meeting. Some of my respondents, however, noted that the portador's official visit was supposed to be a surprise to the family.

At times the portador invited a male friend to go with him. It was the portador's duty to broach the matter of the young man's wanting to marry the daughter of the family and to inform the father of the suitor's family background. For that reason, it was important for the prospective groom to select a portador who knew him and his family well. Typically, the father would respond that he needed some time to think it over and then would respond, ideally, in two weeks. During the visit, the mother sometimes served sweet rolls and coffee to the guests, but she was not usually present during the exchange between the portador and the father. Because the father was the head of the household and the authority figure in the family, he dealt in private with the portador.

The prospective bride was not allowed to be present during the visit. If through some means she learned that her suitor was going to send the portador to speak to her father, she would not let her parents know this.

On the face of it, the mother had little or no role in the decision concerning her daughter's marriage proposal. But after the visitation, the father typically consulted with his wife. As one respondent, a former portador, quickly observed: "Women have always had their say. The wife is always consulted about the marriage proposal and she gives her opinion."

In practice, the father — at least in the 1930s and into the 1950s — talked later not only with his wife but with his daughter. He would ask her if she wanted to marry the young man in question. Then, after the two-week period, the father would deliver his reply to the portador, who in turn would notify the young man and his parents of the decision. In cases where the father did not approve of the match, he might take as long as a year to make his decision. This waiting time served to discourage the suitor and his parents from pursuing the matter. This rejection via indirection was a face-saving device. Also, one respondent reported that in some families it was not unusual for a father who disapproved of a proposed match to avoid discussing the matter with his daughter.

Many Mexican American families believed that if the young man came from a respectable family background and was known to be a good son, he would be a good provider after marriage. His moral virtues and sense of responsibility were usually known to others, especially in the small communities in South Texas. But the portador could not guarantee that he would make a good husband; he could only comment on his family background and conduct to date.

In an instance where the young woman did not want to marry a particular man, it would be the mother who would take an active part in discussing the situation with her daughter. And then the mother would relate the outcome of the conversation to the father. At times the mother would try to convince her daughter that this person was the best choice for a marriage partner because of his good social standing in the community. But, the daughter would not be coerced into getting married to someone she strongly objected to. It should, of course, be stressed that in most of the communities, the girl's family had other sources of information about the young man than what was conveyed by the portador; the latter's visit was often a highly stylized formality.

Again, more emphasis was placed on the young man's moral character than on his economic status. During the 1930s through the 1950s, the vast majority of Mexican Americans were economically disadvantaged. Class differences certainly existed, but for a large sector of the populace, marriage was not a major means of mobility. Under these conditions, a person's status in the community was often contingent on adherence to traditional values — for example, it was more important to be "well mannered" than to carry out a particular occupation.

In general, the role of the portador epitomizes the control the parents had over their daughter's future. It underscores the fact that she was not permitted to make a major life choice on her own. Daughters were protected by parents, especially the father, in order to sustain family respectability in the community. Thus the authority of the father within the family was considerable, and even the girl's brothers had control over many of her actions, especially in public. For example, they would chastise her for speaking to, or otherwise associating with, someone they considered undesirable. Still, this control had limits: the idea of "machismo" can be exaggerated for that era, for the mother was not a passive agent within the family. She had a say in the decision making regarding her daughter's marriage, and she played a major role in socializing the daughter into her new role of wife and mother.

If a favorable decision was reached by the girl's parents, the young man contacted them and requested an appropriate time for a visit by himself and his parents. Upon arrival, the groom-to-be would present a small gift. This second visit (la segunda visita) was to help the two families get acquainted (though the families might already know each other quite well). The young man and the girl were now considered to be betrothed; the couple was not allowed to be alone. In the 1930s and 1940s (and earlier), Mexican American families, especially fathers, were very strict with daughters. Thus, whenever the young man came to visit, a chaperone—a parent or relative—was always present. These strict rules applied especially in the public sphere. Thus the young woman was not allowed to go out in public with her fiancé even after the marriage proposal had been accepted. In the event of a dance, the daughter sat with her family throughout the evening. The young man could dance with her, but he had to escort her back to her seat when the music ended. And the groom-to-be was not invited to sit with her family. One respondent stated that her father would not let her go out with her friends, after consenting to the marriage, because it was not proper behavior for a young woman who was promised in marriage to continue to mingle with single friends or attend social functions unescorted. In other words, after betrothal, the daughter had a special status in the community and was expected to behave accordingly. This reflects in part the "good/bad woman" dichotomy, for a woman who was to be married was viewed as bad if she continued to be seen in public, especially with single males who were not close relatives. In contrast, control over the groom's behavior in public situations was much less.

One elderly respondent observed that during the 1910s and 1920s, some Mexican American families took the initiative in arranging the marriages of their daughters. But this pattern is by no means typical of the traditional culture we are describing.

After the betrothal, the wedding date was set. The husband-to-be at times made monetary contributions for the future bride's daily support—for food, her clothing—until the wedding date. Some families refused to accept the money, however, for they believed that the daughter's support was their responsibility until she was formally married.

As for the marriage rite, it was expected that the young man would defray the cost of the bride's personal wedding expenses, commonly known as "las donas." He (at times with his parents' assistance) would pay for the bride's wedding dress, a lace mantilla or veil, a crown (corona), white gloves, a slip, satin shoes, and the going-away dress. According to one of my elderly respondents: "In the old days, the groom paid for everything. He paid for the dinner too." Another woman told me that her mother's wedding dress had cost $25, but her father had given her $85 for las donas. In the early 1940s this was considered to be a large sum of money, especially for persons of modest means. In some instances, the bride had sufficient money to make other purchases for herself, and she also paid the cost of, for example, a dress for her mother to wear to the wedding.

As for the wedding itself, close friends or relatives of the couple were invited to serve as sponsors, something that was considered a great honor. The sponsors should be a couple who had been married in the Catholic church. The marriage sponsors (who are referred to as godparents for the wedding but should not be confused with the baptismal godparents) carried out various functions. One of the functions of the sponsors was to purchase objects that were symbolic in a traditional Mexican American wedding. These included the wedding cake, the arras, a lazo, the cojines (wedding cushions), and a prayer book. They were presented to the couple at a designated time during the wedding ceremony.

The main sponsors — los primeros padrinos (first witnesses) — were sometimes chosen from the groom's or bride's baptismal godparents or friends of either the bride's or the groom's parents. Again, there were variations on this custom. Los primeros padrinos bought the wedding cake for the bride and groom. Most important, however, they served as advisers both before and after the wedding ceremony. If the couple experienced marital conflict, they could seek advice from their primeros padrinos and the latter would offer suggestions as to how the conflict might be resolved. Still, these wedding godparents did not play as important a role in the couple's lives as the latter's baptismal godparents.

Arras are thirteen coins that were blessed by the priest during the ceremony. They symbolized the fact that the husband would be the provider (though there are other interpretations, such as that the arras would bring the bride and groom good luck during the marriage or serve as an assurance that the couple would never be without money). The lazo, a rosary placed around the bride and groom at a certain point during the ceremony, symbolized the marital bond or the union of the two persons into one. The wedding cushions were used by the bride and groom to kneel on while they received communion during the wedding ceremony. The cushions and the rosary served to reinforce the deeply religious significance of the wedding bond.

In addition to the sponsors, the wedding party included a maid of honor, who typically was the bride's best friend or close relative (e.g., a sister or first cousin). The bride-to-be invited three to five of her friends to be bridesmaids (damas) and each of them invited a male escort (chambelán). Two pajecitos (a little girl who strewed petals from a small basket of flowers and a little boy who carried the wedding rings on a cushion) also made up the wedding party. The groom-to-be invited his father or best friend to be best man. (There were variations on this pattern; for example, a number of weddings did not include bridesmaids and escorts or the two pajecitos.)

In the traditional Mexican American culture, religion played a crucial function in the marriage ceremony. "The binding nature of the commitment itself, the social reorganization that it signifies . . . and the importance of its consequences in the establishment of a home and the production and socialization of children" (Wilson 1966:16) have made this ceremony of vital importance to the community and to religion in many traditional societies. In the Mexican American culture, it has been an occasion for bringing friends and members of the extended family (e.g., grandparents, uncles, aunts, nieces, nephews, and cousins) together for a joyous and happy celebration. There was an overt display of emotions. Family members often hugged and kissed each other and shed tears of joy during the wedding ceremony because they were happy about the religious union of the newlyweds and the two families. The wedding was an important social bond that cemented familial relationships between the two families and renewed solidarity between the nuclear and extended families.

Some Mexican Americans did not have invitations printed for the wedding during the 1930s and 1940s. Several factors might explain this situation. First, there may not have been a printing press in town. Another reason might stem from the economic situation of many Mexican Americans during this era. Some families were too poor to have invitations printed for their children's weddings; here the custom was to invite people by approaching them directly.

In the 1930s through the 1950s, the wedding ceremony typically took place at about 7:00 A.M. on a Sunday. (Some couples got married in the evenings.) The wedding party entered the church with the sponsors leading the procession and the bridesmaids and escorts and the maid of honor following. They took their seats at the front of the church. The congregation rose when the bride, who was escorted by her father, walked down the aisle. She was joined by the groom at the altar. Seated at the altar were the bride and groom, the primeros padrinos and the best man. The parents of the couple sat at the front of the church with the rest of the wedding party.

Most priests in South Texas were not Mexican American; they were Spanish or Irish. The sermons seem to have been largely conducted in the vernacular language. Yet the readings from the lectionary were made in Latin until the late 1960s, when fundamental changes occurred in the church. The mass and the wedding ceremony typically lasted an hour, but might continue longer if people in the church wanted to receive communion.

After the religious ceremony, the festivities began. It was the custom for the groom to pay the expenses of the food and a dance (though not all families held a dance after the wedding). It was customary for the parents of the bride to have a desayuno de boda (wedding breakfast) at their home immediately after the marriage ceremony. (Often, in the smaller communities, churches were small and did not have a parish hall.) Sweet rolls (pan dulce), wedding cake, wedding cookies (pan de polvo), chocolate, and coffee were served—though again there seems to have been considerable variation in the menu among regions in Texas and according to particular family traditions. Some Mexican Americans, for example, served lunch or supper after the wedding ceremony.

If indeed a lunch or supper followed the wedding, traditional Mexican American food was served; this included cabrito guisado (stewed kid goat meat), arroz (rice), and frijoles (beans). In some parts of South Texas carne guisada (cubed meat in tomato sauce) or pollo en mole (chicken in mole sauce) was served, but some families preferred barbecued beef.

As one might anticipate, the persons serving the food were women. Typically, they were friends — for example, comadres — of the couple's parents or else relatives. It was these women who had helped to prepare the food as well. A family with sufficient economic means might employ a person in the community known to cook for festive occasions. The father of the bride and his friends took charge of barbecuing the beef. Nevertheless, the women performed arduous tasks associated with providing the meal, all the while taking care of the guests and the children.

During the 1930s and 1940s, dances lasting well into the night might be held. One respondent said, "You did not see conjuntos (a Mexican band in which the accordion is the main instrument) [at the dance]. It was an orchestra." But conjunto music was played in some areas. When feasible, the parents of the bride rented a dance hall; the poor danced in the backyard of the bride's home.

### The Funeral Ceremony

We turn from ceremonies involving expressions of joy and happiness to one involving ultimate grief and sadness. Once again, my focus is on patterns in the 1930s and into the 1950s, and as I have noted so often, there were variations in the patterns I set forth even in the South Texas region.

A traditional custom in rural communities and in towns and smaller cities was the use of esquelas (announcements) prepared at the local printer's. These would state the name of the deceased, the time and place of the wake (velorio) and the funeral service, and the names of the survivors in the immediate family (see figure 1). These public announcements were delivered, usually personally, to the homes of friends and relatives within the community. This custom of distributing esquelas seems to have been rather common in many parts of South Texas until the early 1950s.

Another way of informing members of the community of a death was to hang a corona (wreath) or a wide purple ribbon on the front door of the home of the deceased. If the deceased had a place of business, a corona was hung on the door to announce to customers that the owner or someone in the owner's family had died.

Upon learning of the death of a close friend or family member, friends and relatives would send flowers to the family's home. Respondents who

Derramad sobre su alma
el perfume santo y salvador
de las oraciones.

Haz, Señor, que sonriente
contemple tu Faz divina,
gozando de eterna dicha.

Hoy

a las 3:50 A. M. falleció en el Seno de la Santa Iglesia
Católica Apostólica Romana la

# Sra. Braulia G. Williams

a la edad de 77 años, 11 meses, 10 días.

Su esposo D. J. Williams, sus hijas May W. Pineda, Lola Williams, Bessie
W. Villa y Velia W. Cruz; sus hijos Robert Lee, Allen, Walter, Delbert J. Jr.,
y David H. Williams; hermanos José G. Cantú, Catarina G. Byington y To-
masa G. Zárate; hijos políticos Pedro Pineda, Gilberto Villa, Lucía C. Williams, Lupita M. Williams, Basilia C. Williams y Lola V. Williams, nietos y
biznietos y demás familiares, profundamente apesarados participan a usted tan
triste acontecimiento y le suplican eleve a

## Dios Nuestro Señor

las oraciones q' su piedad le dicte por el eterno descanso del alma de la finada
y se sirva asistir a la inhumación del cadaver que se efectuará mañana, a las
5 de la tarde, partiendo el córtejo fúnebre de la casa número 110 de la calle
W. Noble a la Iglesia del Sagrado Corazón donde tendrán lugar las honras
fúnebres y de ahí al Panteón de esta ciudad, donde se despidirá.

El Rosario será en la Agencia Funeraria Howard-Williams
hoy a las 8 de la noche y después el cadaver
será velada en la casa de la finada.

Falfurrias, Texas, Marzo 8 de 1954

Imprenta LA VERDAD Falfurrias

**Figure 1**

were in their 70s and 80s recalled that many of the flowers and coronas were of paper or wax.

Traditionally, the deceased's body was viewed in the home; other preburial activities, including the velorio (or wake), were conducted in the home as well. In the l920s the body was not embalmed. The women prepared the body for viewing in the home. It was placed on top of a table covered with white sheets. Or a large board was set on top of some chairs, and the body was laid on it. Four white candles were arranged to form a cross around the body. Since the corpse was not embalmed, large blocks of ice were placed underneath the table to keep it cold, and the wake, which lasted all night, was conducted for one day only. The burial took place on the following day.

During the 1940s and 1950s, the body typically was embalmed in the funeral home and then taken to the house where the wake was to be conducted. The casket (or coffin) was usually set in the front room because it was a convenient place for friends and relatives to view the deceased. (Some of my elderly respondents still recall the era when a local carpenter made the wooden caskets.) The casket was left open, and the upper half of the body was shown, with the deceased's hands crossed and a rosary between them. A crucifix was hung on the casket facing the deceased. If the deceased was an elderly person, the casket apparently was decorated with purple satin. The color blue was used for a little boy and pink for a little girl. Some caskets were covered with white sheets.

During the wake, the rosary was recited in the early part of the evening. Typically, a deeply religious person who was active in the church led the prayers. In some instances, a priest would lead the saying of the rosary, which lasted about half an hour. It must be recalled that in some rural areas and especially on ranches, churches did not exist, and if a formal recitation of the rosary was not held, the family members and close friends of the deceased would engage in prayer among themselves.

In the traditional Mexican American culture, the wake lasted for a full night. Relatives and friends stayed all day at the deceased's home and at all times someone sat with the body. The fact that it was not left alone during the day or night indicated respect for the deceased. Emotions were expressed through loud crying, especially by the women, and talking and laughing were not permitted in the home when the body was being viewed. Such would have been a sign of disrespect.

The women of the family took care of the children and served the food that friends and relatives had prepared for the mourners. The men were usually outside the house visiting with one another. Their conversations focused mainly on the deceased's good deeds and accomplishments. As evening approached, the men were likely to drink beer and mezcal (an alcoholic beverage made of maguey) outside the home if the weather permitted. They would eat caldo (vegetable soup) and drink black coffee to keep them awake all night. The spatial segregation of men and women during the wake underlined the separate domains of men and women. As in most traditional societies, both men and women gained their sense of identity and self-worth by carrying out the routines and rituals associated with the familial/religious sphere.

During the day of the wake, as well as on the following day, friends and relatives brought food to the home of the deceased. Early in the morning, large quantities of sweet rolls (pan dulce) were set out for the mourners. Then, later in the day, other Mexican American food for the mourners was supplied.

Extended family members and various comadres of the family took a major role in preparing and serving the food. An 85-year-old respondent said, "In those days (the 1930s and 1940s) the people did not eat much after the funeral because they were too sad . . . .. There was a lot of crying and the people were in so much pain because they lost their parents or close relative." A woman in her late 70s reiterated that people (especially women) cried a lot. "People were humble back then and more sentimental." (La gente era más humilde antes y más sentimental.)

Funeral services were held in the Catholic church. If a church did not exist, services were conducted in the home and at the graveside. The Catholic religious tradition or, more accurately, the folk Catholic heritage that evolved in the border region provided the setting within which the funeral ceremony was conducted.

Some of the older Mexican Americans interviewed described some of the traditional patterns in the early part of the twentieth century. For example, after the service, six men carried the casket on their shoulders to the graveyard, while the mourners walked behind. Another pattern in that era was the use of carretillas, which resembled a stagecoach pulled by horses, or else a wagon on which the casket was placed was drawn by horses. Two respondents in their late 70s remembered the owner of the stagecoach that was used in funeral processions in their hometown in 1922. Later on, motor-powered vehicles of one form or another were employed.

Once the casket had arrived at the graveside, a priest (or a respected member of the church) conducted a brief service. And then walked up to an important family member (e.g., the widow or widower) and gave her or him the crucifix that had been on top of the casket. The crucifix is an important symbol of respect and remembrance for the deceased and was typically displayed after the funeral in the home of the person on whom it had been bestowed. Then the casket was lowered into the grave. Some of the loudest crying by family members occurred at this time. The women typically cried more loudly than the men, for they were expected to express the deepest emotions of the family members. The end of the graveside service was a painful moment for the family in that it symbolized the deceased's "final separation" from the living. Members of the family and friends completed the funeral rite by walking past the grave and, as they made the sign of the cross, sprinkling a handful of dirt on top of the coffin.

After the funeral ceremony, relatives and friends reconvened at the home of the deceased and continued to express their grief. In the evening, the extended family members (as well as close friends) prayed together in a novenario (novena). Once again, the women did most of the praying. According to this religious practice, one should pray for the soul of the deceased for nine consecutive nights, beginning with the evening of the first day. (Some families began the novenario on the evening after the funeral ceremony.) An older woman or man who was close to the church led the prayers, which lasted for half an hour. The recitation of the rosary was to ensure that the soul would rest in peace and experience a proper afterlife. The novenario also served the living, for this rite promoted solidarity among the extended family members (as well as friends), and the family in mourning was assured of companionship during the early period of grieving for the deceased. After the novenario, people visited for a time, and often the women served coffee and sweet rolls.

The somber nature of the funeral is underscored by the special clothing worn by the participants. The patterns of clothing during, and especially after, the funeral dramatize the differences in gender role patterns between men and women.

At the funeral, men were expected to wear black trousers, a white shirt, and a black band on the upper left arm. Some also placed a black band around the hat. But the men wore this attire only during the funeral rite. Contrast this with the expectations for women, especially widows. Women of the immediate family typically wore a black dress, black stockings, and black shoes, and covered the head with a black veil (even in the home) for the duration of the funeral rite or longer; in the case of the widow, the mourning period lasted for at least a year. In the 1930s and 1940s, Mexican American women—most notably widows—would wear black clothing for the rest of their lives. Some of my respondents in their 60s, and certainly persons I talked with who were in their 70s and older, remembered their grandmothers wearing the black attire, which included a black sweater (worn over the dress) the year round (even during the summers when the temperature reached 90 degrees or above). Several persons noted that some women became ill as a result of wearing this attire during extremely hot days.

For women, especially widows, wearing black clothing demonstrated respect and loyalty for the deceased. It also signified that the woman's identity was intimately linked with that of her husband (an issue to which I return in later chapters). Wearing black clothing also restricted a woman's actions in public, for the community considered her to be in mourning, and it assumed that her fidelity to her husband should continue even after his death. The dress code also signified that women were expected to be serious, to avoid laughter, in public.

So restrictive were these expectations that in many instances women in mourning did not even go out to purchase groceries, relying on their children or others for this kind of task. And some respondents noted that their grandmothers or mothers kept the curtains closed in order to keep the sunlight out of the house during the mourning period.

Mourners, especially women, visited the grave frequently after the burial. Mexican Americans also traditionally celebrated November 2, el Día de los Muertos (the Day of the Dead).[5] Traditionally, this is the day for honoring beloved departed family members and friends with prayers and services. Then, too, family members went to the gravesite not only to place flowers on it but also to clean up the area around it. While carrying out these activities, they might eat a meal there.

Keeping the gravesite in order typically devolved on family members rather than on the community. Also, in many small Texas communities, Mexican Americans (and blacks) were buried in segregated graveyards, although such segregation was less well defined in some areas of South Texas than in others (Jordan 1982; Grider and Jones 1984).

The funeral ceremony drew the extended family more closely together than did the other ceremonies described, and the intensity of the bond among family members was reinforced by the public expression of grief and sorrow. The mutual sharing of deeply held emotions and the common participation in various activities serve to bind people together.

## Conclusions

I have analyzed the traditional life-cycle rituals that were an essential part of South Texas Mexican American culture during the 1930s and into the 1950s. These rituals, as has been emphasized, linked the nuclear family to the extended family as well as to the fictive kinship arrangements. They also connected the family to the community and reflected the deep-seated religious belief system held by Mexican Americans a few decades ago.

This survey of the chief life-cycle rituals seems to be the first of its kind. Of greater theoretical significance is the fact that our knowledge of these rituals—and the family patterns associated with them—provides us with a baseline for evaluating the changes that have been occurring in the contemporary Mexican American family.

Specifically, the rituals, especially funerals, forged powerful emotional bonds and mutual aid within the extended kinship system. If we examine these rituals carefully, we can also discern significant patterns within the conjugal family. For example, the patterns associated with marriage demonstrate how the expectations regarding control over daughters by the family (especially the father) was much greater than for sons. These rituals also point to the "separate worlds" of men and women and the greater authority wielded by husbands, all the while indicating that the "machismo" image delineated in the literature is overstated.

One final question arises: Why direct so much attention to life-cycle rituals? Why not focus on the work and material world of Mexican Americans? I do not deny the basic significance of the latter. Nevertheless, to disregard the cultural system (within which rituals are of utmost significance) is to overlook an essential feature of family life among Mexican Americans. These ceremonial rites provide us with a fundamental understanding of the traditional familial system as well as gender role expectations, and they are an essential baseline for perceiving changes in the extended family over time, as well as within the conjugal family in the modern urban setting.[6] Thus the data in this chapter are implicitly or explicitly the chief reference point in the analysis of contemporary family life among Mexican Americans.

## Notes

1. For a recent work that uses life-cycle rituals to understand family life and the broader social context in a Romanian village, see Kligman (1988). Her work also contains references to relevant works on rituals that I have not cited.

2. The concept of "tradition" involves people's links with their past. Hobsbawm (1983) implicitly distinguishes between at least two kinds of tradition. He observes, "It seems clear that, in spite of much invention, new traditions have not filled more than a small part of the space left by the secular decline of both old tradition and custom" (p.11).

3. Foley et al. (1988) analyze, using data gathered from elderly Mexican Americans in the early 1970s, family ties in the earlier decades of this century. Their description of gender roles is congruent with my own analysis. Although I doubt whether the family, especially among the poor, was quite as stable as they suggest, their information is useful.

4. I have not treated one life-cycle ritual that is often identified with Mexican American culture, namely the fifteenth birthday celebration (los quince años) for a girl. There were several reasons for this decision. One, I needed to keep the size of the project within reasonable bounds (given my resources). Second, this ceremony is gender specific in that it focuses on young women and only indirectly involves young men. All the other ceremonies I discuss directly incorporate both men and women. Nevertheless, a brief comment on this ritual is in order. It in effect serves as a debut for a young Mexican American girl, who is referred to as a quinceañera (one who has become fifteen). The rite is the parents' way of introducing their daughter to the broader community as a young woman who is eligible for marriage.

Of some interest is the fact that this ceremony is being revived by elements of the Mexican American community. Hinojosa Smith (1988) has discussed the manner in which this ceremony has been reestablished in the Rio Grande Valley in Texas. For segments of the privileged sector of Mexican Americans, it has become a major event.

5.  Waugh (1988) describes the activities surrounding the Day of the Dead in San Antonio in the 1950s and suggests that this ceremonial practice was common in that city at the time. Although she does not discuss life-cycle rituals as such in her treatment of certain ceremonial activities among Mexican Americans in San Antonio, her description at least suggests that up to that time, there were still an integral aspect of the Mexican American culture in a relatively large urban center. Her observations are in keeping with my own interview data.

6.  In one sense I am examining an age-old problem in sociology—the transition from gemeinschaft to gesellschaft, from organic to mechanical solidarity, etc. At the same time, scholars such as Tönnies and Durkheim give insufficient attention to the issue of ethnicity in this social transition. Many societies in the modern world have evidenced a revival of "ethnicity" in the face of the onslaught of urbanization, industrialization, and bureaucratization. Although I confront this problem in the last chapter, it requires a full-scale analysis in its own right.

Chapter **3**    **CHANGES IN LIFE-CYCLE RITUALS
                AND FAMILY LIFE WITHIN THE
                WORKING CLASS**

With the background of the traditional life-cycle rituals in mind, we now examine how working-class Mexican Americans are coming to redefine these activities in the course of everyday life. That redefinitions of these life-cycle rituals have taken place and that these, in turn, have accentuated the decline in the extended family among working-class persons is the major theme of this chapter. In the process, a marked decline has occurred in the structure and meaning of the "fictive kinship system" for family members. Nevertheless, elements of this traditional pattern can be found in contemporary urban settings, and they require examination. Also noteworthy is the fact that the present-day life-cycle rituals are associated with new gender role expectations for husbands and wives in both the extended and conjugal family systems.

To understand the redefinitions of life-cycle rituals we must also analyze the ways in which Mexican Americans are defining their religious beliefs in the context of specific interaction settings. In the preceding chapter I emphasized the integral linkage between traditional life-cycle rituals and the religious belief system. Almost all working-class persons still define themselves as religious, but the particular way in which religious beliefs come to be expressed varies according to the particular life-cycle ritual. More specifically, working-class persons may differ in the meanings they attach to given ritual activities.

Most research on the extended family by American sociologists has focused on visiting patterns or "mutual aid" among relatives (Sussman 1968). Although this is not our main focus, we can perceive changes in these patterns when we analyze them in the context of life-cycle rituals. In the process, we are able to place visiting patterns and mutual aid within a somewhat larger context with respect to contemporary Mexican American family life.

### Background Considerations

Before examining the data on rituals relating to birth, marriage, and death that have been collected in Austin, Corpus Christi, and the Kingsville

41

region, some general issues that bear upon the interpretation of the empirical data require clarification.

In the succeeding discussion I combine my findings on the working class in Austin and Corpus Christi. As noted earlier, I studied the latter city to check and elaborate on my Austin data. While the similarities are far more significant than the differences, the latter are duly noted and discussed when they appear to be relevant. The data on the Kingsville region supplement the findings on the two urban centers; they suggest that the changes described for the educationally and economically privileged working class in Austin and Corpus Christi are not limited to larger urban centers but also appear to hold for less privileged working-class groups in the Kingsville region.

Two other general patterns require special attention before we deal with the rituals themselves. One relates to generational differences among the persons with whom I interacted. Another concerns certain conceptual problems regarding religion in modern society.

### Generational Differences[1]

In the course of my in-depth interviews and participant observation, I focused on couples in the age group 25-50. In part I adopted this strategy in order to make the study manageable. Even so, rather perceptible generational differences emerge. With respect to their memory of traditional patterns, an important dividing line exists between persons in their mid- or late 30s and 40s and those who are younger. This generational division holds for the working-class and professional groups in Austin and Corpus Christi, and it exists among persons with few economic and educational advantages whom I observed in the Kingsville region.

This generational division, however, is not a rigid one. (The pattern is complicated by the fact that I collected data over a period of seven years.) Most of the young couples had some knowledge of traditional life-cycle rituals and were aware that their patterns differed from those of their parents and grandparents. They were often cognizant of the fact that they were being socialized into a different set of role expectations. Their social memory of traditional Mexican American culture was, understandably, much poorer than that of their elders. In contrast to the younger ones, the older respondents (e.g., those in their 40s) had more in common with persons in their 60s with whom I interacted informally during my participant observation.

I would surmise that this generational fault line has resulted from major structural and cultural changes that took place in the 1960s and 1970s. Many sociologists have commented on the social upheaval of these two decades — changes associated with a major expansion in higher education,

the growth in the service sector (and other shifts in the economic order), as well as a basic shift in values and beliefs that resulted from challenges from the "youth rebellion," the women's movement, and protests against the Vietnam war. This period of social turmoil affected Mexican American family life. The existence of a significant gap between generations supports my thesis that Mexican Americans, while they are not becoming assimilated into the Anglo social order, nevertheless are being called upon to redefine their everyday lives in terms of the broader social forces that are affecting the society as a whole.

## The Nature of Religion

Inasmuch as life-cycle ceremonies have traditionally been closely inter-woven with the religious belief system, we need to consider the current relationships of religious beliefs to life-cycle rituals as well as to family patterns. Yet an investigation of these interrelationships necessarily leads to a consideration of the meaning of religion in contemporary life.

Sociologists of religion recognize the difficulties of pinpointing the nature of religion in modern society. Roof (1985:75) captures the challenge posed when he writes:

> Contemporary sociology of religion is frustrated in its efforts to study religious change in the modern world. It is difficult enough simply to document religious change, let alone interpret it. Virtually everyone admits that change has occurred in the twentieth century, yet few agree on the specific patterns or their implications.

I cannot hope to deal with the religious patterns of Mexican Americans in detail (such has not been the primary focus of my research). It is, however, essential to come to terms with the manner in which the participants define religion in the context of life-cycle rituals.

In the main, it appears that in the present-day United States it is difficult to sustain any clear-cut distinction between the "sacred" and the "secular" (Greeley 1982). The rapidity of change, especially change fostered by science and technology, has blurred the historical lines between these areas. Certainly, Mexican Americans in their everyday lives no longer define the world in terms of these spheres in any neat manner (e.g., in the realm of birth control). Almost all of the working-class respondents attend church, and those whom I visited displayed religious symbols in the home (e.g., altars or pictures); and people defined themselves as being religious. But religious beliefs do not permeate all aspects of life. For example, they are not perceived as central in the workplace or in the school (almost all the children attended public schools). The differentiation or segmentation of urban life, which has been fostered by the bureaucratization of modern society, has restricted the influence of religion to particular aspects of people's lives. As a result, people interpret religion in somewhat differing ways. Further, during the past several decades, the Catholic church has been redefining its place in the society, and individuals' responses to rituals have been undergoing reinterpretation. Also, some of my respondents have become Protestants, a relatively rare pattern in many parts of Texas until a few decades ago.

The data regarding the interrelationship of family patterns, life-cycle rituals, and religion clearly indicate that individuals conceive of their religious beliefs as having rather generalized significance. In view of this, I speak of a "generalized religious belief system." It follows that the more generalized religious beliefs are interpreted within the context of specific social interaction, and the ways in which particular respondents define the meaning of life-cycle rituals thus may differ considerably.

### The Baptismal Ceremony

The preceding chapter detailed the salient features of the traditional baptismal ceremony of which compadrazgo (or co-parentage) was a basic element. Almost all the persons who viewed themselves as Catholic, as well as some of the Protestants whom I interviewed, had participated in some kind of baptismal rite, and as we now see, the compadrazgo arrangement has been highly modified.

One conclusion stands out as a result of the field research: Today the compadrazgo ceremony no longer serves to sustain the "fictive kinship system" as it was traditionally defined. Among working-class persons in Austin and Corpus Christi, many of its elements have disappeared or been modified. The same general patterns hold for the Kingsville region, including several small towns about which I have considerable data.

The compadrazgo ceremony (as well as other life-cycle rituals) provides us with an insight into the struggle on the part of many Mexican Americans to sustain aspects of the traditional culture, all the while adapting to and coping with the changes that are an essential feature of the complex urban orders in which they live and work. As suggested above, almost all the Catholics view this rite as essential; yet many aspects of the rituals differ from those sustained by Mexican Americans a few decades ago.

Central to the compadrazgo system was the selection of godparents for the infant. In the past, these persons were almost always close friends; this then led to an extension of one's kinship arrangement. Today some couples continue to select friends, but the predominant set of expectations is for either a mixture of friends and relatives or relatives only, often drawn from the husband's or wife's parents or siblings and their spouses.

Diversity in the choice of godparents is a common pattern among couples. In one family of four children, the parents chose as compadres members of the immediate family for their two older children and personal friends for their two younger children. One couple selected the wife's parents as sponsors, and another couple chose a sibling (and spouse) for their two older children, an aunt and uncle for the third child, and friends for the youngest child.

For the parents, the selection of godparents is not a compelling concern. The comments of one of the women reflect a rather common reaction:

> For the first children, relatives wanted to "baptize" them. For the last child, friends came to ask us if they could be sponsors. We did not ask them. We took the first ones who asked. In that way there are no hurt feelings.

From this point of view, the ceremony serves to maintain some meaningful social bonds with friends or family members. Yet the new expectations with respect to choice of godparents reflect realistic adaptations by couples to their own geographical and social mobility and to the mobility of friends and relatives. Under the highly fluid conditions of urban life, it is more difficult to sustain ties with friends than with relatives. In the communities in the Kingsville region, for example, many children or relatives had moved away to larger urban centers for educational and economic opportunities and thus not only extended family but also conjugal family bonds had become more tenuous. Respondents were well aware of these social forces, even though they did not define them as precisely as do sociologists.

Along with the shift in the choice of godparents has come a redefinition in the expectations regarding the responsibilities of godparents. Thus the obligations placed on godparents have been sharply reduced.

None of the couples who chose friends as godparents assumed that they would take primary or full responsibility for the care of the godchild in the event that the parents died. In fact, they did not expect them to provide any economic support for the children. In the words of one woman, "It used to be that close friends baptized the child. Now they just do it and forget it." Another woman noted that "no one believes in the responsibility of padrinos." Yet a number of parents did expect that the godparents would assist the child spiritually. As one woman commented, "I expect them to see that they stay close to God and to make the holy communion. I think it is important." But others, while holding to this ideal, have reservations as to whether friends as godparents would carry out this duty.

They should but I don't think they would. Compadres are godparents that give the child a faith, but no one carries it out.

When godparents are members of the immediate family rather than
friends or more distant relatives, it is often expected that they will assume
more responsibility on several levels. The idea of godparents as spiritual
guides emerges more fully under these circumstances.

That's why I picked our brothers and sisters. Not that I expect
them to take care of the child and raise her. I expect them to see
that they stay close to God. This is the responsibility of the
padrinos. My mother or sister would do it.

In some instances when immediate relatives were selected, it was
assumed they would care for the child if the parents died. Two persons expressed differing versions of this theme.

Padrinos de pila (godparents of the baptismal font) are very important. I feel strongly about the obligation. If something ever
happens to the parents, the padrinos are responsible to feed,
and educate the children [therefore one should select a relative].

I realize now it was a mistake to choose friends. I was only 17
when I got married. My parents will [take care of them], if it
came down to it.

Nevertheless, rarely are godparents chosen with the idea that they will
care for the children if the parents become ill or die. Immediate family
members who may not be padrinos are expected to assume responsibility
for the children. Another woman observed:

I didn't believe in the padrinos doing it. I never gave it a thought
until two years ago. It would be my sister or his brother.

These comments reinforce the thesis that the immediate choice of godparents is often situationally defined, and on reflection the participants
have had second thoughts about their choice. It is apparent that the family
of orientation of the husband or wife emerges as far more central when
couples reflect deeply on who will care for the child in the event that both
parents die. Younger Mexican American couples, in particular, often do
not think about the future care of their children until they are older and
come to recognize their own mortality.

Also, in Austin, Corpus Christi, and Kingsville, working-class couples
did not make it a point to associate with the compadres or comadres over

the years following the baptismal ceremony. In the traditional Mexican American culture these persons were an integral part of the visiting pattern. But this pattern has undergone fundamental restructuring.

Even in a more symbolic sense the role of godparents has declined. As one woman observed, "No one calls them compadres anymore. My parents called them [the child's godparents] compadres and comadres. It meant a real bond back then." While this pattern does not hold true for everyone, it seems to be an emerging expectation. The earlier idea of compadres being associated with fictive kin has essentially disappeared, and so has the terminology. For example, I have heard on various occasions respondents call a sister "comadre" because she had "baptized" their child. But this occurred only in special situations where the person making the introduction wanted to point out that the person being introduced had a special place in the family's life. In keeping with this pattern, three persons stated:

> Los compadres venían a la casa a comer, tomar, y platicar. Ya no. (The godparents used to come to the house to eat, drink and talk. Not anymore.)

> The respeto (respect) was different then. They were closer to their comadres.

> Ya no es tan fuerte el compadre como antes. Han cambiado mucho los costumbres. (The baptismal ritual is not as strong as it used to be. The customs have changed a lot.)

We turn now to the religious aspects of the present-day baptismal ceremony. The prevailing pattern is that the baptismal rite had a compelling religious meaning for the participants. Some said, "I believe in it." Others emphasized this by observing that they did not care about the celebration (or the socializing) after the baptism — it was the baptism itself that carried meaning for them.

Although the baptism had a religious significance for the participants, the specific meaning it conveys varies considerably among the working class. Only a small subgroup in Austin and Corpus Christi spoke of the baptismal ceremony as freeing the child from original sin.

> To cleanse the soul of original sin that you are born with. I really believe it . . . It erased the mortal sin created by our forefather.

Another variant of the religious belief was that the ceremony introduced the child into the Christian faith or the Catholic church. "You are supposed to initiate them into Christianity" or "introduce them to the church [through the baptismal rite]."

As I probed more deeply into the matter, I also found that the baptismal rite was a means of sustaining a bond with the Catholic heritage.

> That was the way I was brought up. Era la tradición. (It was the tradition.) Es la religión católica. (It is the Catholic religion). I believe in religion. That was the way I was brought up. [It was] customary.

> It was a Catholic religious rule. Part of the tradition. Your child must be baptized. I baptized the first three out of tradition. And the small one because of the love for Christ.

For some of the couples, the primary meaning of the ritual was not religious but a matter of family obligation. Obviously, the Catholic tradition in and of itself had special meaning to these particular persons.

> I'll tell you the truth. It is just a family tradition. At the time I did not know the meaning of baptism and I felt bad about it. It was because our parents told us to do it. We didn't know why. At the time we were worried more about the celebration, our dress, how we were going to look — the material things and not the true meaning of baptism.

We cannot neglect the role of the church in defining for the respondents the meaning of this ceremony. Two processes are at work simultaneously: The church is formalizing and routinizing the ceremony on the one hand, and simplifying it on the other.

One pattern of formalization involves requiring attendance at religion classes of those who have been invited to sponsor the baptism of an infant; in some instances, the parents are supposed to participate as well.

> Now you have to take lessons to learn what it's all about. Have classes now for baptism. The Church wants people closer.

> The religion classes are for the padrinos and parents. The parents sometimes [have to attend].

In some instances, lay persons provide instructions for the parents and the couples who have been selected as sponsors. In Austin, teams of lay people go to the home and give instructions about baptism to the parents and padrinos. As one person noted, "I used to do it for 40 people at a time."

This pattern of moving toward formalization or routinization is reflected in the ceremonies themselves. In one of those I attended in Austin, ten children were being baptized at the same time. I found myself in the awkward position of having to call the priest's attention to one child, who was constantly being overlooked. The oversight may have resulted from the fact that the child was not dressed in the traditional white clothing. Yet the mother, whom I did not know, turned to me and noted that the priest was not remembering to bless her child, and she feared that this was a bad omen.

From discussions with various working-class persons, I learned that the routinization of this aspect of the compadrazgo rite was rather common. One person observed,

> When there are 10 to 13 infants to be baptized, the priest does it faster. You cannot understand his words. He cuts out some phrases. Or the priest does it and forgets it.

Still another said,

> They [the priests] lose it completely with so many babies. It bothers me. It's supposed to be special.

While some persons often spoke critically, others came to the defense of the church.

> Just like you have bad teachers, bad nurses, you have bad priests. Some priests don't want to take the time. But this is not in every church. It won't happen in our church. I don't think that it happens in every church. Some priests want to finish the baptism and the mass in an hour and the congregation wants that too.

Along with this routinization, and the not infrequently large and impersonal baptismal ceremony, other patterns in the church are worthy of attention. In the view of some, the special role has been undermined because the baptism is carried out during regular mass instead of in a separate ceremony.

Still others remarked upon the growing informality of the ceremony and the nonadherence to traditional patterns, but preferred the patterns that they remembered from the past. Two observations illustrate the emerging informality.

> The parents hold the baby and más antes (in the past) the padrinos held the baby. A lot of people take pictures.

> [The church] doesn't emphasize lo blanco (wearing white). Dice el padre—lo que tengan. (The priest says "[Wear] whatever you have.")

Some working-class respondents in Austin contend, with strong feeling, that the priests have been arguing that the fictive kinship arrangements are not really meaningful. Inasmuch as they are not out of keeping with church teaching, many Mexican Americans see the priests as "putting down" their traditional cultural heritage. Most priests throughout the area are not Mexican American and thus have little, if any, memory and appreciation of this cultural tradition.

Thus the church itself—with its increasing formalization and routinization, in conjunction with its tolerance of greater informality—has directly or indirectly supported a decline in these traditions. All of this is reinforced by the tendency of the priests to downplay traditional Mexican American cultural traditions.

Still another integral part of the baptismal ritual has been the celebration (typically at home) after the church ceremony. I wanted to uncover what, if any, links the compadrazgo ceremony has to the maintenance of extended family ties.

If we use the ideal expectations of the traditional ceremonies as a guide, we see a marked decline in the size and elaborateness of the celebration following the baptism. More important, today few, if any, extended family members attend.

The typical pattern is for a small group of friends and immediate family members to get together.

> For all of them [the children] just the immediate family came. We had the customary Mexican American thing—pan de polvo (wedding cookies) and cake. Mostly traditional.

> We always had a party for all of them—cake, chocolate, chicken. No one was invited but the padrinos.

> We took the padrinos out to eat. We didn't have a family or home celebration. It seems that the tradition around here [Austin] has changed. Except in one instance, the parents rented the church hall. There was music, food and about 200 people attended. The padrinos threw money from their pockets out to the children outside the church after the baptism. I didn't know about it before. It is called "bolo." To this day, I don't know what it is for.

One woman reported that over a hundred people attended her eldest daughter's and youngest son's baptismal celebrations. For the middle child, however, the couple took the sponsors out to eat at a restaurant. Another woman noted:

> Big celebration for the oldest. Invited lots of aunts and uncles, grandparents. For the rest of the children it was a small celebration. Maybe the grandparents came.

Numerous other instances were encountered where special treatment was accorded the first-born, with smaller celebrations being arranged for the succeeding children. One important factor, of course, is the cost of these celebrations. The members of the working class were cautious about spending money on the party that followed the baptism.

My observations and interviews in Austin and Corpus Christi (as well as in Kingsville) support the generalization that postbaptismal parties are no longer a means of binding the extended family together. This does not mean that from time to time grandparents or other relatives are not in attendance. These persons are far less likely to be present than in the past, however, and they are also less likely to attend the baptismal ceremony than perhaps weddings and certainly funerals.

### The Marriage Rite

I was curious before I entered the field as to whether, and in what way, the traditional arrangements for marriage ceremonies had survived. I assumed, and rightly so, that the use of portadores (see Chapter 2) had disappeared. Still, a number of couples remember their parents telling them about the role of this intermediary in their marriage a few decades earlier. Moreover, a portador had actually helped arrange the marriage of a few couples (now in their late 40s) whom I interviewed. In one case, an uncle had played this role; in still another instance, a padrino de bautismo (baptismal godparent) did so; and in still another case, a well-known person in the community had represented the husband-to-be at the time of the marriage proposal. As one husband observed,

> My uncle went to ask for her [my wife's] hand in marriage for me. I didn't go because I thought that was the thing to do because of tradition.

Another woman, who grew up in a small town, spoke of the role of the portador in her marriage:

He was very well known. I think he asked half of the town.
Everybody would go to him. He was my father's friend.

Another couple reported that the husband went with his padrinos
(baptismal godparents) to ask for the woman's hand in marriage. The wife
said that her husband wanted to contribute to her economic support beginning on the day the parents gave their consent to the marriage; however, her
mother refused the offer on the grounds that this tradition was no longer
practiced. Nonetheless, one husband said: "Desde el primer momento que
te decían que sí (From the moment they told you yes), you had to start supporting her. I sent her a little gift (when her father approved of the marriage
proposal)."

In the case of a small number of couples, who did not have a portador,
the young man's parents would be invited to accompany him when he came
to propose marriage. One of the wives observed:

When we were going to get married my husband's parents came
to talk to my parents. I was in the kitchen listening all the time.
They asked if we would put a plazo (a hold) on the marriage. If
they don't think the marriage will work, they set a date a year
from the day they came over. We didn't do this.

In these negotiations, the participants indirectly say no by postponing the
decision.

The practice of using intermediaries has all but disappeared today.
Many persons indicated that the practice of using a portador was obsolete.
A number of respondents in their late 30s and in their 40s indicated that
they had heard about the practice but that it had no symbolic meaning for
them. In contrast, most younger couples had never heard of the practice at
all. Today the young man goes alone to inform the young woman's parents
of the couple's plans to marry. Here again, we are reminded of a pattern
mentioned earlier, namely, the rather sharp generation gap that exists even
within the group of couples aged 25 to 50 who were the focus of attention in
this research.

The comments of the working-class couples point to the breakdown of
parental control over children's lives (especially that of daughters).
Although children are surely influenced or controlled by their parents, the
traditional dominance patterns have dissolved. The reactions to this by
parents (especially fathers) is one of ambivalence: They are striving to adapt
to the tension between their memory of and commitments to traditional
role expectations and the reality that new role expectations are being
created.

As for the wedding ceremony, most of the couples in Austin and Corpus
Christi (as well as in Kingsville) had been married in a church. A minority of

the respondents had a civil ceremony, although a few of these noted that a few years later they had gone through a church wedding. Most working-class couples view a church ceremony as an essential foundation for marriage. The women strongly asserted:

> I wanted a church wedding and nothing else. We were expected to do what was right. We are not married unless it is through the church.

> I think it is more important to be married through the church than through a judge. It is blessed and has more chance for survival — it's a new beginning.

The responses of the men were similar:

> Yes, it [the ceremony] is religious because I wouldn't marry through a judge. I believe we are together until God comes for us.

> Yes, marriage is not just a piece of paper. It is under God. In 1964, when I got married, it was just a marriage, but it now includes God.

> La iglesia (the church) no te casa (doesn't marry you) just because you want to get married. I had to learn the Catholic prayers [before I got married].

The latter response suggests a subtheme that arose from the statements of working-class couples. As some of them have grown older, they have conceived of their marriage vows as having greater religious significance today than when they got married.

In keeping with the religious commitment of these couples, they conceive of a church ceremony as preferable to a civil one. This is true of persons who married in a civil ceremony and even those who claimed that they did not attach any special religious significance to the marriage rite. Several factors seem to be involved here. A civil ceremony, as a number of respondents made clear, often has a stigma attached to it. For, in some cases, the couple married without the approval of their parents; in certain instances they eloped, in others the woman was pregnant, and so on. One woman complained about her younger sisters' failure to have a church wedding. She disapproved because they were too young (15 and 16); but they were marrying in order to get away from parental control. She felt that her parents would have been far more disapproving if she had acted in this manner, but over the years they had become more flexible with respect to their younger daughters' actions. The parents had been influenced by their interaction with other couples and their own children, and they realized, on reflection, that in the current environment they had only limited control over their daughters' behavior.

Overall, it is evident that the religious ceremony lends legitimacy to the marriage even when couples do not view themselves as devout. That the Catholic church has become less rigid in its expectations (some parish priests will marry women who are pregnant) may help to sustain people's commitment to the church and encourage them to have a religious ceremony. Although this is not a typical pattern in the Mexican American community or in the Catholic church, the respondents have witnessed its occurrence.

Those who have been married in the church typically have had padrinos and have used such traditional religious symbols as the arras, a lazo, and a prayer book. These were quite apparent to a number of respondents. Close friends or relatives who were invited to be sponsors (here we are not referring to sponsors who were also the baptismal godparents) purchased these items and presented them to the couple during the wedding ceremony. For the participants, these items not only reinforced the religious meaning of the ceremony itself but also provided a symbolic link with the Mexican American heritage. A major reason I investigated the marriage ritual in the first instance was to understand its roles in forging bonds with the extended family. Weddings, as was emphasized in the preceding chapter, once brought together not only friends but grandparents, uncles, aunts, cousins, and the like. But only for a relatively small subgroup today do weddings temporarily unite the extended family in any meaningful social sense.

I attended a wedding of a working-class couple in Corpus Christi that underscored the shifting role expectations regarding marriage. I had been acquainted with some of the people who were intimately involved in the wedding. Upon arriving at the church, I was surprised to find that numerous members of the bride's extended family—aunts, uncles, and cousins—whom I assumed would be present, had not shown up. They had been invited, but chose not to attend. Later I was asked by mutual friends and some relatives of the bride if I had seen certain other relatives (such as uncles, aunts, and cousins) at the wedding. I told them that they had not appeared. They were taken aback that close relatives of the bride who lived in the area had not attended, and they were sorely disappointed that I could not convey news about relatives whom they had not seen for a number of years. They had a sentimental attachment to the extended family; yet they would not actually go to the trouble of attending the wedding or otherwise seeking out relatives. Here an emotional bond to traditional extended familial ties was not translated into action.

Afterward, I asked persons who had attended the wedding about this situation. I concluded that for many extended family members, a wedding is not as meaningful today, as either a religious or a social occasion, as it was only a few decades ago. In the traditional culture a wedding was not only a religious event but a major form of entertainment and a means of sustaining solidarity.

While the aforementioned pattern is typical, other kinds of interaction are pertinent. When persons marry without their parents' consent, wedding receptions become irrelevant. In other instances, no real extended family exists. That is, the extended kinship group of some members of the working class is essentially nonexistent. One woman observed: "My sister is my whole family." Another said she did not have first cousins on either of her parents' sides of the family.

A few weddings are large (over 300 persons), but most are much smaller. Yet, even at large weddings, extended family members may not be in attendance. When I inquired about this, different persons commented on their families' considerable mobility. In other instances, they emphasized that in the past families used to be closer. A relatively small subgroup of couples, however, spoke of weddings and funerals as being the last significant connections to the extended family. Several respondents commented:

When a family member gets married, we make it a point to go.

[I go] to see relatives at weddings and funerals. It's awful to say, but it's true. Everyone has his own life. It's so hard [to visit each other]. [We're] too busy.

In the past, people were busy because they worked extremely hard. But the routinization of a bureaucratized modern urban environment means that work proceeds within the context of structured time frames. Wives work, husbands work, and children attend school. And because of the segmentation of various activities, the time frames of family members may not coincide. This makes it difficult even for one family to synchronize their activities so that the members can attend a wedding together.

In part as a response to the routinization and segmentation of urban life, weddings have been simplified. At one time they were all-day affairs, with music and dancing long into the night. A few working-class couples continue to spend a considerable amount of money on wedding receptions, which sometimes includes hiring a mariachi group to entertain the guests. Nevertheless, the length of the reception has been reduced, and the amount of food and beverages likely to be served has decreased. While women still are expected to cook and serve the food, some working women have detached themselves from this kind of activity. They simply do not have the time. Also, many working-class couples face the reality that elaborate weddings are expensive, and they choose to spend their income in other ways.

Traditionally, weddings were, among other things, a form of recreation. They provided relief from the drudgery of everyday life and an opportunity to visit with friends and relatives. Nowadays, television, the movies, and travel may be far more exciting to family members than a wedding. This fact saddens some persons because they feel that family obligations should come before anything else. (I have heard teenagers protest over having to attend weddings.)

Overall, the wedding ceremony continues to have a generalized religious meaning for working-class couples. But its function in sustaining social interaction within the extended family system, except for a minority of persons I encountered, has become relatively insignificant.

## Funerals

Not unexpectedly, a number of patterns associated with traditional Mexican American funerals have disappeared or been transformed. Attending funerals of relatively close extended family members was almost a mandatory expectation in the traditional culture. But just how have traditional expectations been restructured in the light of changing circumstances in modern urban centers?

Esquelas, the printed announcements of a person's death that were distributed to relatives and friends, no longer exist. In fact, most of the younger couples in Corpus Christi had never heard of them. "What we are accustomed to are holy cards with the information about the deceased, and these are given out at the funeral home." Still, a few respondents in their late 40s remember hearing about esquelas.

Not only have esquelas disappeared but also the custom of placing a corona or a purple ribbon on the front door of the home of the deceased has become less frequent. In a few instances, a wreath might be placed on the door of a place of business that the deceased owned, but this practice is rare today (though I have seen it in the Kingsville region during the 1980s).

Today the body of the deceased is not kept in the home, although some persons in their 40s still remember when this was done. The body is taken to a funeral home, and the resultant formalization and commercialization of the funeral rite have affected the way family and friends interact after the death of a loved one.

The all-night wake, so common in traditional Mexican American culture, no longer exists. Instead, a rosary is recited in the funeral home, and afterward family and close friends may reconvene in the home of the deceased to be with the immediate relatives. Also, saying the rosary at the funeral home is usually limited to one evening, for it may cost extra money to keep the body there longer.

While the traditional wake has largely disappeared, family members, especially the spouse of the deceased, may stay at the funeral home during the day to sit with the body. But many respondents noted that when the funeral home closes, people are expected to leave. This has greatly restricted the amount of involvement of family and friends with one another before the burial. Thus we see that nowadays working-class people are expected to pray and express their grief in accordance with the "bureaucratic time" of the funeral home and the workplace.

A number of Mexican Americans, especially those in their late 30s or 40s, reflected upon the many changes that have occurred.

> It was a lot of crying. It was very sentimental. It was a lot of comfort for the family. Más antes (in the past) las tías lloraban (the aunts cried). Not today. I don't believe in it.

A woman indicated:

> The older generation is used to praying a rosary for the dead and they wear black longer. My mother wore black for a year when her mother died. All her clothes were black. I remember we couldn't turn on the TV and radio. Now it is different. Life goes on.

Part of the decline in the degree of emotion displayed in the funeral home, in particular, can be attributed to the latter's social expectations.

> Most mexicanos (Mexican Americans) tend to stay with one funeral home and that funeral home takes it for granted and they think they can do what they want to do with the people. They do not let us have our traditions. We have to be out at a certain time. It is impersonal. It is very different today. I don't like it.

In Austin (as well as Kingsville) I encountered people who observed that the funeral home associates had chastised Mexican Americans for crying too loud, claiming that it was disturbing to other persons.

Sociologists in recent years have rediscovered emotions, but they seem to downplay the fact that many kinds of emotions, including those associated with death, are constrained by the organizational setting in which they are expressed—in this instance, funeral homes. Thus the routinization and impersonality of urban life, in keeping with its increasing bureaucratization, channel how and when grief is expressed by both Mexican Americans and Anglos, whose lives are so intertwined with modern bureaucratic structures. The latter impinge, often in little understood ways, on very intimate aspects of everyday existence.

Along with the loss of emotional intensity is a concern, especially among persons in their 40s, with the loss of respect for the deceased.

> Funerals are a sad thing. The trend is to go out and not be lonely. This is not Mexican culture anymore. I don't like people talking, laughing in front of the body. They should go outside. People laugh like it was nothing. I don't like that.

Although there is a deep-seated concern by many working-class persons over the loosening of emotional bonds at funerals and a lack of respect for the deceased during the funeral rites, funerals today are not devoid of religious meaning. But the religious meanings are by no means similar to those in the traditional culture that held sway a few decades ago. The Catholics and the subgroup of Protestants I encountered in Corpus Christi and Austin (and the Kingsville region as well) conceive of funerals in religious terms. As one said:

> Funerals always have religion. It is the last thing we are going to do for the deceased. You go out of respect for the person who died.

> Mi deber es de ir (It is my duty to go). I also put religion in front of it. A lot of people don't like funerals, but it can't be helped. Yes, they are religious.

A few working-class persons, primarily men, downplayed religion in their discussions with me. But when I probed about this, it became apparent that they too hold some general religious beliefs, and they too expect their relatives to arrange a religious-type funeral for them. While it was somewhat unclear just what religion means to them, there was no question that they expected some religious funeral rite led by a priest to be held for them. This was part of their taken-for-granted world, and these data support my thesis that Mexican Americans are increasingly coming to hold to generalized religious beliefs, which come to be interpreted in accordance with new circumstances. (This trend is more well defined for the professionals.)

As for the religious ceremony, it has become somewhat simplified, and the graveside atmosphere is no longer as somber as it once was. But during the funeral at the church and at the graveside, loud crying by the women is no longer heard. Although women still appear to be the chief mourners, their role is by no means as prominent as in the past.

After the funeral, there is a social get-together. But certain traditional patterns have been modified. A typical comment on the part of women is:

> That's the only time we see relatives that we haven't seen for a long time. They are happy to see one another (translated from Spanish). They are talking, joking. It's like a little reunion. But it's because they haven't seen each other in a long time. It is more socializing. I used to think it was a bad place for it, but not anymore.

The men echoed these sentiments:

> [At funerals] that's most of the time when we see our relatives. We exchange phone numbers at funerals and everyone promises to call but no one does. Then we see them at another funeral. We are happy to see each other. The neighbors bring food and pan dulce.

> There's a lot of sentiment but calmer now. Now you go to a funeral and everybody's outside drinking beer, talking, getting acquainted. They are happy. About a year and a half ago I went to a funeral. I got to see my aunts, uncles, cousins, and grand-mother who I hadn't seen in a year or so. The only time they get together is at weddings and funerals. What starts out to be a sad thing turns out to be a joyful thing. But when you get close to el cuerpo (the body), they get quiet. We talk about the good times. Some people make it a celebration. They [relatives] won't come for vacation. Now some people are doing family reunions.

The social gatherings after the funeral proper are no longer as somber. Many persons, particularly those in their late 30s and 40s, were deeply disturbed about the loss of respect for the deceased. They are torn between a longing for tradition and a recognition that times have changed. Today, the familial and friendship gatherings turn into a party—a time when relatives and friends who have not seen one another in years can reminisce and discuss the divergent paths they have taken in life. But the social-gathering-like atmosphere is difficult for many persons to accept. As one woman stated:

> After the funeral, we went to my mother-in-law's house to eat. Everyone brings food. Our relatives would start to lift everyone

by saying jokes or all that little stuff to make you forget the funeral idea. We were happy to see people — relatives we don't usually see.

Funerals, even more than weddings, are the last major means that members of the extended family have to forge links with one another. This theme came up time after time. Both men and women noted:

Weddings and funerals are times when you see everyone. We never have time to see them otherwise. We go through the same promises of calling. It's a shame to do it, but we do. We are so busy with work. We are sad and happy to see one another.

If it wasn't for a funeral or wedding, we wouldn't see our relatives. Really, the funeral is a get-together for the family. It kind of takes the pain of the sorrow away because of the get-together.

Some working class couples met members of the extended family for the first time at a funeral and the social gathering held afterward.

My cousin from West Texas came. When my mother died, a niece whom I had never met came. It's strange, but that's the way it is. That's when I realized that I had more aunts and uncles that I had never met. I was stunned to know how big the family was. Alot of aunts came from out of town. People come more to funerals than to weddings to pay their last respects.

Still, not all funerals serve to forge social bonds between the nuclear and the extended family. The comments of a subgroup of persons bear this out. Two women expressed themselves in the following terms:

My Dad's only brother lives in California. I don't go to my cousins' funeral out of state. I did not go even when my husband's mother died.

On my father's side, there's no one left. No cousins, no sisters, no nephews. We never met his side of the family. Not even my mother knew them.

The observations of two men are in the same vein:

Two months ago, I went to my brother-in-law's funeral. I didn't really know him. I went because of my family. We don't visit. They have never come to Austin.

Lately the funerals of my relatives are out of town, and I can't
go. I am working, and they are too far away.

Along with a decline in the emotional intensity associated with the
wake, the funeral ceremony and the social gathering afterward, other
changes have taken place in the postburial rituals.

Only a handful of members of the working class in Austin and Corpus
Christi reported that they attended novenarios for the full nine nights. It is
far more common to attend only a few or none at all (for, in effect, it is no
longer a meaningful element of the funeral rite for certain members of the
working-class). Unlike the situation where persons were concerned with the
loss of respect for the dead in the immediate postfuneral social gatherings,
the decline of this traditional form evoked no real sense of loss. As one
woman expressed it:

> I'm sure my parents had novenarios. I didn't attend any, and I
> did not have one for them [when they died]. I am not in favor of
> them.

Another response was: "Eso lo hacían más antes" (They did that in the
past). Of greater interest (especially to certain social scientists who have
stressed its role in characterizing Mexican Americans) are the women's reactions to mourning. The older tradition of women wearing black after the
death of a husband or parents is not part of the expectations of working-
class persons (both men and women):

> My mother wore black for a long time when my sister died. She
> never used lipstick or make-up again. [She] could not attend
> celebrations at all. I didn't do it.

> We don't have time to have traditions. Nobody mourns for a
> year or more. I remember women wearing all black. I did it for a
> few months but not like before when you wear the long black
> dress. I wouldn't turn on the TV or radio.

> After my dad died she [mother] wore black, everything — shoes,
> nylons, slip, dress, veil — for three or four years. I finally got her
> out of it.

> I remember the black band around their [men] arms. This cer-
> tified that a relative died. A ribbon around a hat too. I
> remember that.

One of the implications of this redefinition of role expectations is that within the lifetime of respondents in their late 30s and 40s, a major shift has occurred in the manner in which women comport themselves after the death of a husband (or, at times, parents). Except for a few men who expressed some sense of concern that the tradition of wearing black had changed, no one ever talked about bringing it back.

While the more extreme forms of mourning that were once part of the Mexican American heritage have disappeared, this does not mean that elements of tradition have not been sustained to some degree. But the mourning patterns have undergone reinterpretation, often in response to the demands of contemporary urban life.

> I do it for respect. I don't listen to the radio for seven days or after they have been buried, I don't want arguing or loud talking [in the home].

> When people die, if it's a friend, I don't listen to music for three days. If it's a relative, it is for two weeks.

> I did it. Not going out for awhile. If I went out, I wouldn't tell my mother where I was because she would get mad.

Also in the discussions of mourning there is a tendency by some working-class persons to articulate the growing privacy within which mourning is carried out. A woman expressed it well.

> Hay dolor (there's pain), it's private now. La gente nunca está conforme (The people are never satisfied). If you use luto (mourning), they still criticize you. If you don't use it, they still don't like it.

So, too, with men, who at times spoke about the private nature of mourning. It is not that they are not sad, but they do not express their grief in a public manner. This also means that the solidarity that comes with public mourning over the death of a close relative has declined very sharply in the past several decades among Mexican Americans who live in urban centers of Texas such as Austin and Corpus Christi. Similar expectations are emerging in the Kingsville region as well. The modifications in the postfuneral rites with respect to the Day of the Dead (November 2) appear to be quite dramatic. Although on this day some members of working-class families still place flowers on the graves of relatives to honor the deceased, the activities associated with the Day of the Dead have been losing their religious significance. In communities such as Austin, the Day of the Dead seems to be turning into a "modern celebration" with a decidedly secular ring. In one instance, a variety of social activities followed upon "a downtown parade, led by a white hearse decorated with paintings of skulls" (Pinkerton 1988). Many persons in their 40s and older react quite negatively to this redefinition of a once-sacred tradition that paid homage to the dead. What is significant here is that the newly created activities have no necessary relationship to family activities, especially the honoring of deceased family members (cf. Hobsbawm and Ranger, 1983).

## Conclusions

This chapter has surveyed the basic changes that have occurred in the traditional life-cycle rituals of working-class persons in Austin and Corpus Christi (as well as in the Kingsville area). In all the communities studied, the general patterns are much the same. Through examining these rituals I have made a number of points concerning family life. For example, the fictive kinship system viewed as typical of Mexican American culture by some social scientists has been modified in ways not recorded in the literature. Moreover, as far as baptism and marriage ceremonies are concerned, these no longer serve to bind together the nuclear and extended families. Only funerals remain as the major means of keeping extended family members together, and the structure even here is more fragile than in the past. This is no minor finding, for scholars such as Sena-Rivera (1979), Keefe et al. (1979), and Keefe and Padilla (1987) insist that the extended family is still an integral part of contemporary Mexican American life. I discuss the implications of my findings for current generalizations about the Mexican American family after I treat life-cycle rituals within the business/professional group.

## Notes

1. Karl Mannheim (1952) was one of the first major sociologists to call attention to the importance of "generations" in the study of a social order. However, Skolnick (1987:366-71) has outlined some of the difficulties associated with the study of generational differences in family life in contemporary social orders. Some of the generational differences are not so well defined as in many traditional societies.

## Chapter 4

**CHANGES IN LIFE-CYCLE RITUALS AND FAMILY LIFE WITHIN THE BUSINESS AND PROFESSIONAL CLASS**

Having examined the changing patterns regarding life-cycle rituals among the working class, we turn our attention to how these rituals have been reshaped within the business/professional class. (I often simply use the term "professional.") While the general patterns regarding these changes are similar to those within the working class, a separate analysis of changing patterns within the professional class is warranted. First, the data emphasize the fact that changes in the kinship system in the contemporary urban setting are such that we can no longer speak of *la familia* as a central aspect of Mexican American culture (cf. Sena-Rivera 1979; Keefe et al. 1979; Keefe and Padilla 1987). While not all ties with the extended family have been severed, we find that, using the traditional patterns as a baseline for our analysis, there has been a major decline in the interaction among extended family members in recent decades.

Second, by elaborating on the restructuring of the relationship between the conjugal family and the extended family within the professional class, we find that certain patterns differ from those in the working class. Although the class differences in the kinds of familial system changes are less for the extended family structure than for the conjugal arrangement (see Chapters 5 and 6), certain patterns were uncovered that have not been documented by other researchers. Two in particular merit attention. First, the professional class's religious belief system is of a more generalized sort than that of the working class. Thus the professional couples' interpretation of the meaning of rituals affects, and is affected by, the shifting nature of the belief system. Second, one segment of the professional group seems to emphasize keeping the rituals alive more for reasons of tradition than to sustain religious beliefs for their own sake.

In discussing these patterns we also elaborate on theoretical issues associated with the decline of rituals and revisions in family arrangements.

### Background Considerations

The preceding chapter explored why changes in ritual patterns are significant for understanding revisions in the extended family system.

Traditional rituals have been associated with the sacred tradition and with the maintenance of sacred time. Persons in the professional group no longer rely on rituals as a means of sustaining a sacred link to the past, and there has been a marked decline in the social or "collective" memory that many members of this group have of traditional cultural patterns. At the same time, the sacred and the secular are intricately linked in actual practice (cf. Greeley 1982).

Further, by examining the main life-cycle rituals — those associated with birth, marriage, and death — we are able to see the Mexican American family within its broader community context (the family does not function as an isolated unit, even in the urban setting). We want to understand some of the linkages between the family and community and the religious belief system as we turn to an analysis of specific life-cycle rituals in the Mexican American professional class.

### The Baptismal Ceremony

As mentioned earlier, one reason the baptismal ceremony has been singled out for study by social scientists is that within the traditional Mexican American culture it led to the creation of a "fictive kinship system" called compadrazgo, one in which the extended family came to include not only members of the kinship system but also persons who were close friends.

It is apparent from both the in-depth interviews and other fieldwork data that the patterns associated with the baptismal rite (and the compadrazgo relationship) have been restructured in fundamental ways within the professional class in Austin and Corpus Christi. More and more, couples are selecting padrinos (or godparents) who are relatives rather than friends. More specifically, couples either select only relatives or a mixture of relatives and friends. Nevertheless, as in the working class, the diversity in choice of godparents is considerable. The least frequent pattern is adherence to traditional expectations in selecting only friends as padrinos. In both Austin and Corpus Christi it was common to find couples who selected friends for the first or second child and relatives for younger children. For example, one couple with four children had chosen family friends as sponsors for the two oldest children, the wife's sister as sponsor for the third child, and the wife's brother as sponsor for the youngest child.

In both communities the choice of godparents (padrinos) was not a major issue. The comments by one woman typify the expectations involved in selecting padrinos:

> They [our parents] had more friends than relatives as compadres. We're not so much into compadrazgo because they [the

baptismal godparents for our children] are our brothers. So it isn't compadre, let's do this and that. In the past, baptism was more important, especially in small towns. It is a social event for people like my parents, and they take it more seriously.

One reason the choice of godparents is not a major consideration is that couples who have selected friends as godparents do not assume they will have any essential responsibility for the children. If the godparents are close relatives, the responsibility is felt to be especially great. The crucial factor is that these persons are close relatives, not just godparents.

Some members of the working class still see padrinos as playing some role in the religious upbringing of children. Within the professional group, the responsibility of padrinos is rather vague. The parents want the padrinos to be good friends to their children. Nevertheless, a number of couples (especially those in their late 30s and 40s) commented that their children had lost all ties with their padrinos, except where they were close relatives. One male respondent spoke for others when he said, "For many years we kept in contact, but then we didn't see them for years."

The reactions of parents when asked about the responsibility of godparents indicate how far they have moved from certain traditional patterns. The wives stated:

> As far as I'm concerned, I don't think I would expect them to [help] because my family is very close. I expect my brother to do that. It [the baptismal ceremony] was more like a social. Although the church says that we have responsibility as godparents, we don't take it literally.

> My sister. That's why we chose her. I don't believe in the church's tradition of responsibility. That's asking too much.

> We thought it out. We picked relatives. Someone had indirectly offered but we had already made a deal.

The husbands' comments were similar to those of the wives:

> They have no responsibility, even though culturally that is what they are accepting. I have my brother as legal guardian.

> My parents or my brother or my wife's brother and sisters would take over. Regardless of what the religion says, I feel strongly about that.

I would like for the family to take over. That's why we chose our immediate family to baptize them. Usually the grandparents or the sisters take over. We are a very close family.

I don't count on it for other people. It would be a relative, but we haven't assigned it [the responsibility] to anyone.

To reiterate: Relatives are becoming more important in the baptismal ceremony because the parents do not expect friends to care for the children in any significant manner. They hope that their children will stay in touch with their godparents, but even this expectation is often not realized. The parents themselves may have few, if any, long-standing ties with their compadres (co-parents) if they are only friends. The traditional cultural pattern whereby compadres and comadres socialized and interacted intensively with one another is practiced today by very few members of the profes- sional class. Thus one person observed that "the compadres do not go out drinking. There is no time for that." Regular socialization among com- padres who are not relatives no longer seems to exist in the social memory of most Mexican American professionals and is certainly not carried out in practice.

As for the religious meaning of compadrazgo within the professional class, we must preface our analysis with a brief discussion of certain dif- ferences in the patterns in Austin and Corpus Christi. One is in the religious orientation of members of the professional class. The couples in Corpus Christi are typically more faithful churchgoers than those in Austin. Even church attendance can be somewhat misleading as an indicator of "religiosity," however, for those who attended church frequently were not as devout as were members of the traditional Mexican American culture. Moreover, they are not as devout as older persons with whom I have interacted in the Kingsville region, for these persons come closer to perpetuating the older beliefs and practices. For them, the realm of the sacred is pervasive.

In practice, we find two kinds of religious patterns within the Mexican American professional class. One can be labeled more religious than the other (with the qualifications noted above), and proportionally more of these persons live in Corpus Christi than in Austin. The second, less com- mon, type (not found in the working class) has a more generalized belief system. Some of these couples even deny that they are religious (this is especially true of the husbands). We cannot always accept their initial com- ments at face value, however, for they qualify this denial in various ways. The existence of this second type suggests fundamental changes in the belief system of a segment of the Mexican American group, and this in turn is reflected in the manner in which the life-cycle rituals are interpreted.

Within the more religious sector of the professional class, women interpreted the compadrazgo arrangement in the following terms.

> It's a sacrament. Have to make sure they have all the sacraments.

> To me, baptism is registering him with God. It is the point in time when parents realize that the child must be raised as a practicing Catholic.

> We have to educate our children, and show them the meaning of the Catholic church. Baptism is the first contact a baby has with the church. They have to know their roots.

The men spoke in a similar vein:

> The parents take an active part in the religious upbringing of the child. Baptism is the first step. It is to initiate a child into the faith.

> Introduce them to the church. This is their first contact with Christianity.

Although this religious theme stands out, it was also true that only a small segment of the professional class emphasize that baptism is essential for ridding the child of original sin. Their link with the church and with their Catholic heritage is central to the respondents' interpretation of the meaning of the baptismal rite. One woman spoke for this small group as follows: "As I understand it, baptism is to become a member of the Catholic faith and to do away with original sin." A man observed, "If something happened to him [my son], he is baptized. We were more in a hurry because my niece was in a coma. We realized how important baptism was in case something happened to him." Still, the lack of emphasis on original sin, even by persons who view themselves as strongly committed to the church, suggests a break from traditional expectations.

Among the less religious sector of the professional class, Mexican Americans, in reflecting upon the religious significance of the baptismal ceremony, assert:

> I have not thought about it until the interview.

> No, not really. I think it has more of a social gimmick to it. You go with the padrinos to have supper.

No. It is an expected part of the ritual.

Never thought of it, we just have to do it if you're Catholic.

These comments point to an emerging pattern that deserves special attention. A number of couples in the professional group are seeking to sustain these ceremonies as part of their cultural heritage, not because of any strong religious conviction. The ritual is part of the Mexican American tradition and has only a vague religious meaning for those participating in it. The emphasis on tradition is more compelling than religion itself. Significantly, such a pattern did not emerge from my observations of the Mexican American working class. Also, unlike many members of the working class, those in the professional sector (except in rare instances) do not attend religious classes. And, in general, changes in baptismal practices are not stressed in the professional class. Some persons noted that the mother holds the baby during the ceremony, whereas it once was the madrina's responsibility. And Latin or Spanish is no longer used in the ritual. Many members of this group were also reflectively aware of the fact that, as one woman observed,

We live in a highly mobile society, and we have our own agenda. We move around more and we are no longer in a rural setting. That makes the difference.

As for the celebrations after the baptism, these too have lost their historical significance. The majority of professionals stated that they were not interested in elaborate festivities. If they prepare a meal at home, they usually invite members of the family of orientation of the husband and wife and some close friends, if the latter are compadres.

The respondents' voices convey a strong sense of how they have defined the situation. The women indicated

For the first one, we went to eat in a restaurant. For the second one, it was nothing special.

For all four of them we went out to eat or we ate at home. I don't feel comfortable with any kind of celebration. I never made a big thing out of it.

[The celebration is] not big. We didn't invite other people. Just his parents, my parents. It wasn't a big dinner for any of my children. We're not into that.

The men spoke in generally the same terms.

> We went home and had a dinner prepared by my wife's parents. For all four [children], our grandparents, brothers and sisters came.

> Ten to twelve family members got together. We always have something but not big.

> My mother had some cake and punch. Just us, the padrinos and my mother. No big affair. No big celebrations in our generation.

There were only a few professional persons in Austin and Corpus Christi who reported that they had had a big celebration for their children's baptism. One woman remarked that the celebration for the first-born had been spontaneous, whereas the celebrations for the two younger children were planned well ahead of time. About thirty guests had attended the get-together, and this was considered a large gathering. Several other persons reported the same patterns.

Among the professionals, as among the working class, the baptismal ceremony no longer serves to bring together members of the extended family in any meaningful way. It is not just that the fictive kinship system has largely disappeared—except in broad symbolic terms (which should not be ignored)—but that the baptismal rite no longer serves to integrate the conjugal family with the extended family and with members of the community at large.

### The Marriage Rite

As the subtitle of this book emphasizes, we are concerned with the role of tradition and with change. As we have by now come to expect, in the Mexican American professional group many traditional features associated with life-cycle rituals have disappeared or undergone basic revisions. This is true in the role of the portador. Still, one couple in their 40s who earlier had lived in a small community had used a portador. According to the husband, "My brother-in-law and the husband of my first cousin went to her [my wife's] house. They spoke to her mother, and she told them to wait for six weeks. They then came back and the answer was yes."

Many respondents in both cities had heard of the term portador or were familiar with the custom. For example, after I explained the meaning of the word, one woman said, "My grandfather was a portador. He asked a

lot of girls to marry the boys. I didn't know what to call it, but he did that."
Another offered, "This is the first time I have heard that word, but my
brother-in-law used someone to come and ask for my sister's hand in marriage. I remember it was his uncle; I was very little then." There is thus a
social (or collective) memory of this traditional pattern, but the practice, as
such, no longer exists. This change, as we have stressed, has been dramatic,
having occurred within only a few decades.

While the use of the portador has disappeared among younger couples,
some aspects of this traditional form had been practiced by the older
couples (typically those in their 40s). As one member of the professional
class observed, "My husband and his parents went to ask for my hand in
marriage. His father did the talking. My father told them to come back in
two weeks." This same woman reported that her sister's boyfriend had asked
a friend to speak to her father about the marriage proposal and that her
father ran him off. He wanted the young man's parents, not a mere friend,
to approach him. In the case of some older respondents, the husband had
had his parents accompany him to the young woman's home when approaching her parents about asking her hand in marriage.

Nowadays, couples first decide to get married and then either announce their plans to their parents or go through the formality of asking the
young woman's parents for permission to marry. Parents do not control
their daughters' lives as they did in the past. For example, several men spoke
to this issue:

> I went to her house and we just told both of them [the parents]
> that we wanted to get married in a year. I was very direct with
> the announcement.

> I asked for her hand in marriage over the phone. They were ex-
> pecting it. They lived out of town.

Or, as one woman put it, "We all sat in the front room, and Ruben told
my parents that he loved me and wanted to marry me." The couples themselves decide to get married, but often they want at least the tacit approval
of their parents.

With respect to the wedding ceremony, a small group of respondents
had been married in a civil rite; most had been married in the church.
Primeros padrinos (first witnesses) are still an essential feature of the
ceremony. There is also a maid of honor, a best man, and sponsors for the
lazo, the arras, and a prayer book. Often there are four bridesmaids, and
some couples invited two pajecitos (a little boy who carries the wedding
rings and a little girl who drops flower petals along the church aisle).

According to a number of respondents, some couples today invite numerous sponsors as members of the wedding party. This is a recent phenomenon, and it is frowned on by some members of the professional class. As one woman complained, "They [the parents] want their friends to pay for the wedding."

In general, close friends and relatives, most often members of the nuclear family of the bride and groom, are invited to be sponsors. As one woman indicated, "We had all our brothers and sisters at the wedding." Still, we find variations on this theme. "My husband invited his roommate to be the best man. This is unusual. My sister was my maid of honor." Another woman reported that she had sponsors at the wedding but that she took care of all the costs. She said, "I was a little modern. I had the madrinas (sponsors), but I bought everything."

Within the business and professional group, only a few women (but no men) emphasized the traditional meaning attached to such objects as the lazo and the arras. A number of the couples had included these items as part of the wedding ceremony, but the traditional interpretation of their function has been lost. They were incorporated because this is the way Mexican Americans carry out their weddings. Among a number of couples, the continuation of certain practices seems to be for reasons of tradition, not because of any inherent religious meaning attached to them.

Couples who attempt to adhere to features of the traditional wedding sometimes find it difficult to do so. Several respondents observed that not all priests are familiar with the meanings attached to objects such as the lazo and thus need to be reminded by the participants (often the sponsors) just how these should be incorporated into the ceremony. Thus, even if Mexican Americans are committed to maintaining certain religious traditions with respect to marriage, the institutional structure of the church may not support their actions. As noted in the previous chapter, very few priests are Mexican Americans, and often they have little interest in sustaining the cultural heritage of this ethnic group.

With respect to the religious significance of weddings, there is a division: Some persons are rather committed to religious practices, whereas others downplay them. According to a male respondent in the first category, "I believe it's religious. I never wanted to get married any other way." Still, an ambivalence about the religious dimensions of the marriage ceremony is reflected in the words of one professional woman: "It's religious because we grew up thinking it's important. I guess the spiritual aspect is important." Some persons whom I interviewed did not see any religious meaning to the marriage ritual. Even a few persons who were involved in a variety of activities in the church did not stress the religious aspects of the marriage rite. This was not an uncommon reaction within the less religious sector of the professional group.

Overall, to members of the professional class, the religious meaning associated with social interaction in the marital rites is less compelling than that associated with baptisms and funerals.

As for the reception following the wedding, the patterns vary considerably. The small minority of couples who had a civil ceremony typically did not hold a reception or party afterward. Those who had a church wedding did hold a reception. What is striking about these receptions is their diversity, not only in size but in other features as well. As for size, three groups can be roughly delineated — those with about 25 to 75 guests, those with 100 to 200, and those with 200 or more. In the case of large-scale weddings, the marriage ceremony carries with it important status overtones. Nevertheless, none of the weddings within the professional class today is the all-day affair that we associate with traditional Mexican American culture.

The professional couples were aware of this diversity. I have attended a number of weddings during the past decade not only in Corpus Christi and Austin but also in other communities in Texas, and I, too, have been struck by the varying nature of these gatherings. A sizable group of couples had music and a dance as an integral part of the reception. But this is by no means a dominant pattern. There also seems to be little standardization in the food served. Although Mexican American food is typically available, it is not viewed as essential for the maintenance of ethnic identity. Moreover, in a number of instances the food was catered; here the women of the families involved did not take the lead in cooking and serving the food, a sharp break from tradition.

As suggested above, weddings and the receptions that follow are generally not a bridge for bringing the extended family together. Only for a small minority of Mexican American couples did weddings serve this function. According to one woman, "Cousins get together and it's fun. My cousins have small kids and we like to visit." In the words of another woman, "We try to go to first cousins' weddings. It is impossible at times because of his [my husband's] work." Only one couple mentioned that members of their extended families had attended the wedding and had assisted them in financial and other ways with the reception.

Typically, more friends than relatives attend the wedding. One male's response was common. "The tendency is to invite close friends of the bride and groom, rather than to make the family the focal point. In the old days the family was the focal point, but this has changed today." There is no evidence from my research that marriage rites are a vehicle for furthering interaction among extended family members. Social and spatial mobility, the demands of the work world, and financial costs (among other factors) have all led to a break in the linkages between the marriage ritual and the participation of members of the extended family as well as the broader community.

## Funerals

It is very apparent that within the professional group the interaction associated with funerals has been fundamentally altered (again using the traditional culture as the basis for evaluating social change). For professional persons, the collective or social memory regarding esquelas highlights, as it does for working-class respondents, the generational gap between persons in their late 30s and 40s and those in their mid-20s to mid-30s.

A number of the older respondents knew about esquelas. Some of them had seen them.

> I remember as a young man going out to distribute them. The immediate family put the names of friends and relatives on the esquela. My mother did it when my father died.

> A long time ago, I remember seeing them. We had a newspaper, but it came out once a week. We had esquelas.

These Mexican Americans had grown up in small towns before moving to urban centers. One of the more unusual observations was made by a Corpus Christi woman who a few years earlier had seen an esquela attached to a Dairy Queen in a small town north of the city, and her husband had asked her what it was.

Among the younger members of the professional class, few had heard of esquelas. One respondent in Corpus Christi asked her father if he had known of esquelas, and he remembered seeing them in a small town south of Corpus Christi in the 1950s but had no recollection of their use in Corpus Christi proper during that era. When I used the term esquela, most of the younger respondents wanted to know what it meant. They had never heard of it. Because the esquela is a tangible item, it dramatizes just how rapid has been the loss of social or collective memory regarding certain features of the traditional Mexican American culture.

The professional persons also took note of the decline in the use of coronas (wreaths) at funerals. They are not part of contemporary funeral rites within this group.

As for the funeral rite proper, today the body is taken to a funeral home. Even so, a few persons remember, a time not long ago, when the body was viewed in the home. Although nowadays the deceased is viewed at a funeral home, the wake still exists, though in diminished form. The immediate family members take turns staying at the funeral home during the day and evening to sit with the body and receive friends and relatives who come to pay their respects. Family members are asked to leave when the funeral home closes.

The rosary is still said in the evening at the funeral home. Reciting the rosary takes about twenty minutes; either a priest or someone else who is deemed deeply religious leads the prayers. Some friends and relatives remain for an hour or two with the bereaved.

Respondents in Austin and Corpus Christi, especially those in their late 30s and 40s who remember more traditional funeral patterns, emphasized that the wake is much less somber than it used to be. Here are typical comments by men and women.

> It is solemn, quiet—there are no emotional outbursts. There was crying but it was quiet. The family sat in the front rows and they were crying softly.

> I remember the crying but people don't do it anymore.

> There is not as much open crying. I remember we could hear the sobs. The funeral home takes over. You can't even see the family.

As with the working class, in the professional group a number of persons spoke in varying ways, about the commercialization and formalization of funeral rites today. This pattern is associated with the fact that displays of emotion are more and more a private matter. Mexican Americans still express grief, but this is done more quietly than before. Too overt a display of emotion is frowned on in the highly impersonal setting of a funeral home.

Along with this increased sense of privacy regarding the notion of grief, there are fewer flowers at many funerals. If the deceased is socially prominent, flowers may play an important role. But in many cases they do not. Some families request that their friends give a donation to their parish instead of sending flowers. Still others prefer to dedicate a mass in honor of the deceased at a later date. Patterns are evolving that were unknown in the traditional culture.

As for the religious meaning of funerals, we found that some of the same divisions within the professional group that were discussed with respect to baptism. One group, more heavily represented in Corpus Christi than in Austin, still regarded funerals as having special religious significance. (Even so, these persons were by no means as devout as were

Mexican Americans steeped in the traditional culture.) When asked whether funerals had special religious significance, some of the women replied as follows:

> Yes, it is significant because the person is going to heaven. I don't know exactly what it means, but you feel she [he] is going to heaven. That is what the religion says, and it makes you feel secure and good.

> Yes, they have some religious significance. Personally, I think that it is the only ritual that should be taken seriously.

> Yes, because we always take the body to church. Our religion keeps it from becoming impersonal. It gives us a chance to say good-bye. I know someone who got cremated and there wasn't a rosary. We didn't feel like we said good-bye.

The men also spoke in these terms. One man observed that, after his father's death, "My mother kept the crucifix — porque es un recuerdo del muerto (because it is a remembrance of the deceased). My mother has it in her bedroom and she prays to it. It is important."

The second group disavowed any deep religious commitment, but when pressed they admitted that they too want a religious funeral, especially a mass. Nonetheless, their belief system is highly generalized, and at times ambiguous. Thus, when queried about the religious meaning of funeral rites, the women in this group responded as follows:

> It makes you feel good. Completes the ritual. But [it's] not religious for religion's sake.

> It's kind of an expected thing at funerals.

> Funerals are not important, and we rarely attend them.

As for the men,

> I don't think so [that funerals are of religious significance]. It is part of the ceremony. Depends on whether you are religious or not. I'm not.

> It doesn't have the same meaning anymore. The priests are not that interested, I think. Well, I guess they go to so many and it's not their relatives.

Some of the ambiguity in the religious interpretation of funerals is perhaps more fully captured in the comments of one woman:

> I guess it is of some religious significance to me. But it is not as important as other ceremonies that pertain to the living. I don't believe that when you die you go to hell if you have been bad. We pray to God and ask Him to alleviate the pain for the living.

The expression of doubt concerning the religious meaning of funerals in one sector of the professional group has no counterpart among the working-class persons I encountered in my research.

The shifting nature of religious beliefs among professionals (even those who regard themselves as religious) means that these persons do not engage in the same intensive personal interaction with family members and friends that Mexican Americans did some decades ago. The intense emotional drama of funeral rites brought family members together in ways that are lacking in the wake and the funeral service today. The traditional funeral rite created a social solidarity within the extended and conjugal families that is not replicated in modern urban centers (cf. Durkheim 1915).

This brings us to other aspects of the social interaction associated with funerals, namely, the social get-togethers after the graveside ceremony. These differ greatly from those in the past. Today, Mexican Americans in the professional group do not assemble just to mourn the dead but also to visit with relatives and friends. Comments by both men and women support this social fact.

> Everyone went to my mother's home. People brought food. It was more like a family reunion. Everyone got together—like people from out of town. My mother was really entertaining people.

> It's time for recollection. Funerals have changed a lot. It becomes a social gathering. It is not as sad anymore.

> Funerals are more of a social type thing—a socializing event. You feel it's a time to draw closer to each other, and you are happy.

There is a lot of socializing at funerals, a big change from the past. But not everyone fully approves of what is occurring.

> I don't approve. They went home, talked about it [the funeral], drank beer and entertained the people who came. I approve of the social get-together, but not the beer.

Rosaries nowadays are used for the purpose of catching up on the latest news — socializing. I feel very uncomfortable with that shift because the passing of someone is a sad occasion. It is inappropriate to be talking, laughing. Everything has changed in this respect. There's too much socializing because we do not see each other. But it doesn't have to be that way in the funeral home. But the old times — I'm not too sure that was good either. The men are outside drinking and reminiscing.

Funerals continue to serve another major function for a sizable sector of the professional class. It appears to be the last major event that brings the extended family together. Throughout my interviews and participant observation, the special link of funerals to extended kinship ties came to light. The women noted:

I have been to funerals mainly to see relatives. That's why we go back to the house [of the immediate family of the deceased]. We talk about the good old times. People bring food. We eat and talk. I have a lot of relatives that I don't see [except at funerals], or I meet a relative who has never come before.

It is the last time to offer respects. It is final. Everybody comes from all over. People won't come from Laredo or San Antonio for a wedding, but they will for a funeral.

We see relatives at funerals. That's the time to see them. They all exchange addresses and promise to call each other or to stop by when they are in town. But it doesn't happen. They wait until there's another funeral.

I went to a funeral and met relatives I didn't remember or never knew. People were telling me how I fit in. Some of them I remembered from childhood.

The men's views are similar:

It should be weddings first and then funerals in terms of seeing relatives and friends, but it doesn't happen that way. [Why?] People think a funeral is more important than a wedding because you'll never see that person again. And then you never see that family. First cousins don't keep in contact. They have their families. I never see mine.

> I just went to a funeral and I saw the extended family. People I
> hadn't seen in a long time. I feel more obligated to go to a
> funeral than a wedding.

For another sector of the Mexican American professional class, even
funerals do not bring the extended family together. Therefore, some
couples in the professional class seem to have lost ties with most elements of
their extended kinship system. For the social scientist to analyze mutual aid
among extended family members is a rather fruitless endeavor when a
significant sector of the professional group does not see their extended kin
except at funerals. Those who stress *la familia* as an integral part of the
Mexican American culture are not considering recent happenings within the
more socially and economically advantaged sector of Mexican Americans.

As for postfuneral ceremonies such as the novenario, these too have
been disappearing. I met only a few persons — two men in their late 30s and
early 40s and one woman in her 40s — who had attended a novenario for all
nine consecutive nights. Only a small minority seem to attend the first few
nights of the novenario. Some respondents reported that they are unable to
stay for the novenario because they live out of town and have to return to
work. By implication, most persons in the professional class do not attend
the novenario at all. Many younger persons in the study had never heard of
the practice. This holds true even for those persons who attend the Catholic
church regularly.

As we might expect on the basis of the data presented above, the traditional mourning rite in which a widow wore black for the rest of her life is
no longer part of Mexican American urban life. The change in this realm
has been dramatic.

Among women, the following observations are relevant:

> The only significant death was that of my father. I didn't have
> any mourning. It was a sad and difficult time for me. At the
> time I was going through a lot of changes myself.

> I didn't mourn according to tradition. My mother did for a
> while, but not to the extreme.

> My husband's grandmother died wearing black all her life.

The views of the men are typified by such remarks as these:

> Mourning [such as wearing black clothing] is not used anymore.
> I feel that rather than mourn we should pray.

Sure you do something [i.e., grieve], but wearing black for a year or not going to the movies for a certain period of time [is no longer an expectation].

I picture her [my great grandmother] in black because that's all she wore. She wore a black veil over her head and long black dresses. In every picture I saw she was wearing black. I haven't seen any other pictures so I don't know what she wore before. As a matter of fact, I haven't seen very many pictures. I don't know why. Maybe they didn't have film.

While Mexican Americans in their late 30s and 40s still have a memory of the traditional cultural definition of the role of women, as reflected in their actions after the death of a husband, they have broken from the expectations of the traditional culture. In addition to the mourning patterns, other postfuneral customs have declined. Women once took the lead in perpetuating the ceremony associated with the Day of the Dead (November 2), but professional women today have no commitment to doing so. (As noted earlier, this ritual is now being reinterpreted as a "secular" rite by some Mexican Americans in certain urban centers.)[1]

## Conclusions

This chapter and the preceding one have focused on revisions in basic life-cycle rituals. Although the patterns for the working class and the professional classes are similar in many respects, some rather striking differences also appear. Perhaps the most significant is that relating to the religious belief system, which in the traditional culture both supported and was supported by the life-cycle rituals. This system has undergone basic revisions. The churchgoing sector of the professional group is less committed in its religious beliefs with respect to everyday activities than are members of the working class, and the other professional group has an even vaguer and more highly generalized belief system.

Although many facets of the rise of a generalized belief system in the religious realm cannot be explored herein, the existence of this phenomenon merits attention. Sociologists have in recent years lent relatively little attention to the relationship between religion and family life (cf. D'Antonio and Aldous 1983). That the religious beliefs of Mexican American professionals have become more abstract means that these persons can, in carrying out their everyday activities, more freely interpret their religious beliefs so as to accommodate them to new situations in which they find themselves. Many professionals are quite flexible in the manner in which they interpret church doctrine so as to fit special circumstances that arise. One result is that role expectations for professional women are not as constrained by religious beliefs as for working-class women (and especially for women in the traditional culture). This is reflected in how professional women have been remaking their roles with respect to life-cycle rituals (and in other areas as well).

In a more specific sense, the emergence of generalized religious beliefs goes hand in hand with the restructuring the life-cycle rituals. These rituals are no longer a means of sustaining the solidarity of the extended family. Still, funerals are the one last effective link that many professionals (as well as members of the working class) have with extended family members such as uncles, aunts, and cousins.

Other patterns merit attention. In both the working class and the professional class a rather sharp break is found between persons in their late 30s and 40s and those in their 20s and early 30s regarding their collective memory concerning Mexican American culture. A major rupture with tradition has occurred during the past several decades (cf. Schultz et al. 1988). This loss of social or collective memory of many features of traditional family life (as reflected in life-cycle rituals) has been fostered by the mobility associated with urbanization and industrialization. It has also resulted from the fact that with urbanization, industrialization, and bureaucratization, the institutional support for sustaining a memory of the traditional culture has been undermined. The community, the church, and the schools do not help to keep the memory of certain traditions alive. (My analysis of social or collective memory is based on the premise that the mind is social in nature, and it is the social mind, not the social self, that sustains a memory of the past.)

Although I have described the loss of social memory regarding many aspects of traditional culture associated with life-cycle rituals, I would also emphasize that various elements of the traditional culture persist. That a sector of the Mexican American professional class continues to adhere to many cultural traditions even when these have lost their religious significance provides us with a basis for correcting certain misunderstandings about Mexican American life today. It is a major error to assume that the loss of a social memory about certain aspects of traditional culture (e.g., life-cycle ceremonies) is accompanied by a loss of ethnic identity. Instead, this ethnic identity is being redefined. As an instance, the fact that contemporary funerals have been sharply revised should not be interpreted to mean that Mexican Americans are becoming like Anglos. Anglo funeral patterns have also been drastically revised in recent decades. How can Mexican Americans be emulating new sets of social expectations that are still in the process of emerging? I return to the theoretical implications of these phenomena in the final chapter.

## Notes

1. The revival of the Day of the Dead as a "secular" rite, and the renewed emphasis on the "Sweet Fifteen" ceremony (Hinojosa Smith 1988) mentioned in Chapter 2, note 4, deserves future research. In view of these patterns we can speculate that Mexican Americans will reestablish various elements of traditional life-cycle rituals as one means of ensuring ethnic solidarity within the urban setting.

Chapter **5**    **ROLE MAKING AND DECISION MAKING WITHIN THE WORKING CLASS**

This chapter moves from a consideration of changes in the extended family to an examination of revisions in the conjugal unit, with an emphasis on role making and decision making.

Two contradictory conclusions regarding decision making between husbands and wives are expressed in the social science literature. One is the importance of "machismo" as an all-encompassing form of male domination. The other is the egalitarian nature of the relationship between husbands and wives.

A number of ethnographic studies have portrayed the Mexican American family structure as strongly patriarchal (Madsen 1964; Rubel 1966), a view that continues to be perpetuated by well-known social scientists (Queen et al. 1985). Mexican American men have been described as adhering to an ideal in which manliness (machismo) is equated with authority, strength, honor, bravery, and sexual prowess. It is the husband who makes all the important decisions in the family. The wife defers to him, and by implication she gains her identity through being married and through being a mother.

In contrast, a recent body of literature on decision making in the Mexican American family argues the opposite: Decision making in the Mexican American family has been seen as increasingly egalitarian in nature according to Hawkes and Taylor (1975), Cromwell et al. (1973), and Ybarra (1977, 1982). These studies have relied heavily on the theoretical orientation and research procedures of Blood and Wolfe (1960), who contended that decision making between husbands and wives results from their differential control of strategic resources (in effect, this is a variant of "exchange theory"). Blood and Wolfe, and others utilizing their orientation, have collected their data through closed-ended questionnaires. Such a research procedure does not enable us to uncover the processual nature of decision making.

Zavella (1987) observes that neither the patriarchal nor the egalitarian model is adequate for interpreting the working-class Mexican American family. I would agree. Nevertheless, her research, significant though it is, looks at conjugal relationships primarily through the eyes of women. Also, because her focus is on women in the workplace, she approaches the family from that perspective. Herein I examine the orientations of both husbands and wives, beginning with the family setting and moving out to the work-place and the community, in an attempt to determine how this broader setting affects conjugal relationships.

I am intent upon casting the issue of conjugal power relationships into a social context broader in scope than that of other research. There is now a vast body of literature that seeks to assess the power relations that exist between husbands and wives with respect to decision making on specific issues, for example, the purchase of a car, or the disciplining of children. Even so, McDonald (1980), among others, has observed that our understanding of conjugal power relationships leaves much to be desired, and he suggests that alternative approaches need to be explored. Most of the research has been carried out from the perspective of some version of exchange theory. But this orientation has definite limitations for understanding how husbands and wives arrive at decisions. The processual nature of decision making (including the give-and-take of negotiation) is typically overlooked. In part this is because most of the research on decision making has employed closed-ended questions, and it is almost impossible to track social processes over time with this methodological tool. Of even greater theoretical import, apparently no student of the family has examined the decision-making process within the context of role making. We know that husbands and wives in the broader society have for some decades been remaking their roles, and in the process they have been redefining each other's influence and power (Hertz 1986; Gerson 1985). In a more general sense, no one seems to have placed specific decision-making patterns within a broader interactional context and, in line with this, interpreted the nature of the power relationships between husbands and wives. This is what I propose to do in this and the succeeding chapters.

## Perceptions of Change Over Time

In order to provide a contextual understanding of the ongoing redefinitions of power relationships within the conjugal family, we need to know how husbands and wives conceive of their own decision-making arrangements — whether they are similar to or different from those of their parents.

Only a small handful of the working-class Mexican Americans I interviewed or observed during my participant observation assumed that their marriage relationships were similar to those of their parents. And these persons were men. The great majority of wives and husbands took it for granted that significant changes had occurred between the generations.

Working-class couples, especially those in their 30s and 40s, were quick to note that their parents lived in a different era: They had less education and less money, and they led a harsher existence. Often, working-class persons saw a "causal" relationship between the way their parents acted toward each other and their deprived economic circumstances.

The respondents spoke in pointed terms. One woman stated:

> It was a different era. My family lived on a ranch y la vida era más dura (and life was harder). He [my father] didn't believe in having things—a house and furniture weren't important to him. After all, we never had any money.

Another indicated:

> Economic. We have it better and my kids got a running start. My parents were poorer, but they had skills.

Analogous comments were made by men:

> I think my father and I are two totally different persons. I am better off because I have this and that, and he never got us anything. My parents were poor. My mother was very limited because she did not go to school. My father made the decisions because he earned the money. But they didn't have enough money for the bills.

> I think it is different now. No one got educated in my family. As for my parents, no tenían dinero en el banco (they didn't have money in the bank).

In general, husbands and wives perceived the father as the most powerful figure in the household. The observations by a number of women reflect the overall orientation regarding the relationship between husbands and wives in the past.

> Years back it used to be the man. He made all the decisions, the women had no say so.

> My mother praises my father too much. He doesn't do it and she gives him credit. My mother is old fashion.

> My mother se quedaba en la casa (stayed at home). She had no voice in family affairs.

> There is no comparison, because he [my father] decided everything.

> They live in a small town and they are more traditional. That's the biggest difference. I am more aware of the family and the shortcomings. In those days they were very strict . . ... We showed a lot of respect for our elders. We still have it — respect — but it's more casual.

Again, often the working-class men spoke of the strictness of their fathers. These comments suggest that working-class couples do not see themselves as like their parents.

Still, the aforementioned comments must be placed in their proper context. While many husbands and wives defined their parents' relationships in terms of the dominance of the father, they were using their own situation as a standard. Other observations made by working-class persons indicate that a significant number did not view their mothers as passive. Thus, the women took note of their mothers' role in such comments as these:

> My father was the authority figure in the house and we respected him but he was considerate of my mother. If it was late, he would tell her to stop or tell us [my sisters and I] to help my mother.

> My mother took care of us. He went drinking or working when we were small. As far as I can remember, my mother made the decisions. She is very smart even if she does not have an education.

> My mother was the boss. She used to do everything. My Dad brought the check and she did everything. She disciplined us; he never argued with us. She bought the furniture. He was old-fashioned.

These observations are reinforced by the men. For example,

> When it comes to my mother, she showed us to cooperate with our wives. To have respect and trust them. When it came to my father's death, there were a lot of problems. She was lost. The mother is the whole home. A father is only part of the home.

To be sure, some women in the past had become widowed and were forced to bring up children on their own. A number of the working-class persons I encountered spoke of how strong their mothers were, even in another era. "She was a widow and she did everything. My mother had to make all the decisions. My father was gone."

From the perspective of these working-class persons, the family of orientation was patriarchal, but, again, a variety of responses to questions indicate that this dominance was by no means complete. Wives and mothers exerted authority in the private sphere, and if widowed, they took the lead in caring for their families.

### Sex-role Expectations

Sex-role expectations are also relevant for understanding power relations in the family. What a wife or husband is expected to do may have some effect on the manner in which power is exerted. Scanzoni and Szinovacz (1980:42) contend that "traditional sex roles—roles that are sharply different and rigid—tend to make family decision making 'unnecessary' or else quite simple." From this perspective, there are a great many implied understandings between husbands and wives as to what each is supposed to do, and both take these expectations for granted. Although no human interaction is so fixed as to exclude shifting interpretations of these normative expectations, nonetheless, traditional role expectations set broad constraints on how wives and husbands relate to each other—though, as we observe, we must be careful in how we interpret these kinds of data.

What exists among working-class husbands and wives is that they reply in rather traditional terms to questions regarding gender (or sex) role expectations or definitions of their own or their spouse's role. Thus, in the abstract, tradition is a meaningful aspect of the lives of working-class couples. But, in this instance, what they say does not correspond to what they do. Later on, we detail how the role-making process as well as decision making regarding specific issues do not necessarily reflect the ideal expectations as to sex roles among members of the working class.

More concretely, when respondents were asked about general role definitions or expectations (as in the in-depth interviews), they usually replied in traditional terms (see Chapter 2). When they discussed specific decisions, however, they did not necessarily conform to their traditional definitions of sex-role expectations. This pattern should not surprise us. A body of sociological knowledge supports the principle that even though persons talk in one way in concrete situations, they may (and often do) act in another. Deutscher (1973) has documented this type of discrepancy in human action in *What We Say/What We Do*. My data lend further credence to the necessity for carrying out in-depth interviews and engaging in participant observation if one is to understand power relationships within the conjugal family, for all too often the responses to formal questions reflect ideal rather than actual behavior.

Among working-class couples, the wife is expected to care for the children and perform household duties such as cooking, washing, and housecleaning. The husband is perceived as the provider for the family. Over and over again, the following themes emerged in response to questions about what wives and mothers should do:

> I should show my family love and that I really care about them. I should take care of the children, dressing them and sending them to school. I should be a mother when needed—when they're sick or have problems of any kind.

> The kids come to me for love and affection and he does too. He doesn't like to be nagged. He comes to me for support.

> Cook 99% of the time, clean, wash and spank.

The women constantly stressed taking care of the home and their children and being a good wife.

A few women did not adhere to the traditional ideal expectations. "I have to have food on the stove for him. He expects me to get up to cook when he gets home. I did it for years. I spoiled him. The last two years I have backed off."

The women spelled out the traditional male duties and responsibilities in the following terms:

> He should bring in money so that the family does not have to work. He should provide for the family, but also be concerned for their well-being. He should love us and be a father to my children.

> He should provide the money. He should also love his family.

As far as women were concerned, it is quite apparent that men should work, provide for the family, and love their children. In discussing ideal expectations concerning their role, working-class wives gave little, if any, attention to how they should be treated by their husbands.

When we look at the role expectations from the male perspective, we see that these are in keeping with those of their wives. Two major themes emerge with respect to the wife's role. "Bringing up the children is the number one priority." The husband cannot spend a great deal of time with the children because he must work. In addition to caring for children the wife should "prepare the meals, clean the house, do the dishes, and have the clothes ready." One man spoke of his wife as providing "maid services."

With respect to male expectations for themselves, the husbands reiterated many of the views that their wives held.

> I should work and bring in money. I am the provider. I have to
> work to feed the family, to give them what they need. And I
> should be a good parent to my children.

The emphasis was definitely upon the good provider role; it was the number-one consideration. Yet, some men observed that they should teach their children discipline as well as love. And, in some instances, they spoke of providing spiritual guidance for the children.

Only a few men deviated from these ideal expectations. One man conceded that he helped his wife because she worked, but he then justified his action when he said, "We have an agreement — she takes care of the inside and I take care of the outside. She helps me outside and I help her inside."

While the ideal expectations are useful background information, they do not tell us a great deal about how persons come to remake their roles and how they actually reach certain kinds of decisions. Taken at face value, the ideals expressed suggest little, if any, change in traditional sex roles.

## Role Making by Husbands and Wives:
## A Clarification of Issues

We are now at the point where we can uncover the nature of role making by husbands and wives as well as the resistance to this process. But the succeeding analysis requires that we have a clear understanding of the concept of "role making." This in turn leads us to elaborate on some rather fundamental sociological issues.

Ralph Turner (1962) introduced the concept of role making into sociological literature over a quarter a century ago. Although his essay has been widely cited, the idea of role making has been utilized explicitly by only a few researchers in the course of analyzing empirical data. Turner has done so to some extent (e.g., Turner and Shosid 1976),[1] and so has Zurcher (1983). To be sure, many social scientists who have examined the changing roles of men and women in the past two decades have implicitly employed some form of the role-making framework (e.g., Gerson 1985) but they have yet to grasp the theoretical orientation that underlies the analysis of their data.

The basic premise of role making is that human agents take an active part in restructuring, or attempting to restructure, their own roles. Role making is different from role taking. Role taking, which calls for adopting the expectations of others in the course of one's actions, emphasizes social stability. In taking the role of others, human beings tend to act according to how they believe others expect them to act. In role making, however, human beings are not just being reactive; they are also proactive in that they are striving to create new roles for themselves. Role making involves role taking, but role taking does not necessarily involve role making.[2] This distinction is essential to an understanding of how Mexican Americans, especially women, are redefining their place in the social order.

When we consider the role-making process, we are led to give special attention to the "social mind." Most symbolic interactionists have emphasized the idea of the self. Certainly the concept of the self, which is always social in nature, is a crucial one and is part and parcel of my analysis. However, it is because of the social mind, not the social self, that persons are able to engage in social calculations and reflective thought and empathize with others and thus respond to new and complex situations in a variety of ways and create new roles for themselves. The social mind emerges only in the context of interaction with others; one's mind is not a fixed biological entity. How we learn to think arises within the concept of interaction with other persons.

Because of the social mind, persons come to have a social or collective memory. They store past experiences (albeit selectively) and use this memory as they respond to changing social circumstances. Thus, Mexican American husbands and wives have a memory of the traditional role expectations. My stress on the social mind is in keeping with the efforts of certain social scientists to give it greater prominence in the understanding of social interaction (Smith 1982; Vaughan and Sjoberg 1984; Collins 1989).[3]

To interpret the data regarding the actions of Mexican American wives and husbands, we must elaborate on, as well as modify, Turner's formulation regarding role making. Turner stressed that role making takes place in situations that are vague and ambiguous. But we must also realize that human agents create new roles by remaking traditional role expectations (Chapter 2). It is this latter situation that receives major attention in the succeeding analysis. Then, too, resistance to role making occurs—a pattern that Turner did not examine. Thus, empirically, we come to grasp role making by recognizing the resistance to it. Such resistance to role making by wives, for example, is found not only within the familial context but also within the community and organizational setting (McCall and Simmons 1982). My fieldwork experience leads me to conclude that we cannot comprehend the issues regarding role making unless we consider negative reactions to the remaking of traditional expectations concerning how wives (and husbands) should act in everyday life. Again, recognizing the dialectical process between role making and the resistance to it enables us to discern the emergence of new kinds of conjugal relationships among Mexican Americans.

### Specific Role-making Patterns

But just what kinds of role making are occurring among working-class husbands and wives? Social scientists argue that women, especially women in the Anglo middle class, are taking the lead in reshaping their roles (cf. Stryker and Statham 1985). No research reports have delineated this process for Mexican American working-class women. Husbands and wives were very aware that fundamental changes in their relationship with each other had occurred over time. This was particularly true for those who had been married for a number of years. A number of women took the view that the men were not as dominant today as in the early years of marriage. This pattern is highlighted in the comments of one wife who, in discussing her changing relationship with her husband, indicated:

> Whatever he said went like that. I'm not so timid now. I have some say. If I don't like what he does, I'll tell him so. Before we did not communicate with each other. He was a very dominating person, and even my friends noticed this pattern.

The men replayed the themes of the wives. In the early years of marriage, "I said something and that was it." Today, the husbands stress that there is more discussion with their wives.

While changes in the roles of husbands and wives were apparent to the participants, the couples were unable to define just what was going on. Only after a rather extended period in the field did I sort out the fundamental role-making pattern that is taking place among working-class women. Essentially the women are striving to attain a new personal, as well as social, identity for themselves. One's personal identity can be quite private (or personal), whereas one's social identity is public (Weigert 1983). The issue is not equality but the search for a separate identity on the part of the wives.

The wives' newfound personal and social identity sets them apart from traditional Mexican American women. Strikingly, none of the working-class women in Austin and Corpus Christi (and Kingsville as well) expected to follow the traditional mourning patterns if they became widowed. That women no longer sustain a symbolic social identity with their husbands after the latter's death certainly reflects a major change from the past. Moreover, the husbands did not expect them to follow this traditional pattern.

A somewhat separate identity is essential today if a woman is to carry out certain activities within the public sphere after her husband's death. In view of the fragmentation of the traditional extended family, a widow can no longer rely on relatives to shop for groceries or carry out basic tasks for herself and her family. Also, the demands of the workplace do not permit these women to engage in extended mourning rites. Thus they have had to do more than take the roles of others; they have had to reshape, often in a reflective manner, their own roles in the light of the major structural changes that have been occurring in modern urban communities.

But greater specificity is required in detailing this search for a separate identity. For the working-class women, three types of role-making patterns can be delineated. Most of the working-class women reflect Type II, discussed below.

### Type I: A Personal (but Limited Social) Identity

A very few of the women have achieved a personal identity apart from that of their husbands, but they have been unable to translate this into a meaningful social (i.e., public) identity. In their own private way they view themselves as separate from their husbands. But the lack of a broader social network of family, friends, or fellow workers has made it impossible for them to establish the kind of social identity they long for, one that would provide public support for their personal identity.

The experiences of one Mexican American woman serve to illustrate this pattern. During the interviews, she complained that she did not have an ID card issued by the Department of Public Safety. She had heard that she could obtain one, but her husband was unwilling to assist her in this endeavor, and she lacked a network of friends or a kinship system that could help her. She needed transportation as well as assistance in filling out the proper papers. Her lack of social identity had been embarrassing; for instance, she had at times mistakenly been identified as a Mexican national, although she was born in the United States and is a Mexican American.

After a couple of interviews, she asked me to help her secure an ID, and I agreed to assist her. Her husband did not object, in part because I was an "outsider" and in part because of my educational status. After she obtained her ID, she was able, for example, to cash checks, and she was therefore elated with her newfound social identity. The ID dramatizes the need for a separate identity if one is to carry out even minimal activities, such as cashing checks, within the impersonal, public sphere of a contemporary urban setting. College-educated women take these matters for granted.

### Type II: An Emerging Personal and Social Identity

Most of the working-class married women I interviewed or encountered in my fieldwork were in the process of attaining a degree of personal and social identity (i.e., autonomy) apart from that of their husbands. This identity has come to be achieved, and is expressed, in a variety of ways. It typically involves support by relatives, friends, or persons in the workplace. Moreover, it may involve personal achievements outside the home that reinforce the fact that the woman in question does indeed command special skills and knowledge that make her different from her husband. Also, it involves the learning of social skills, including negotiation and image management, that make it possible for a wife to cope more effectively with her husband's resistance to her emerging identity.

First, as to the support system, one of the most crucial kinds consists of older children, especially daughters. In several instances, daughters attending a university in another community encouraged their mothers to visit them. In one case, the husband reluctantly permitted his wife to travel without him, and the wife commented as follows:

> I used to drive all that way to see my daughter. My husband could not go, so I drove it. I was not familiar with the roads, but I did it.

These concrete actions signified the wife's independence from her husband and served as a significant step in creating a sense of her social identity or autonomy.

Thus, daughters who become better educated than their mothers play a role in socializing the latter into creating a new identity, and at times they are able to intervene with their fathers and persuade them to become less rigid in their expectations.

Second, the development of a personal and social identity depends not only on a support system but also on the attainment of new social skills and knowledge.

The newfound identity of these working-class women is given credibility by their special knowledge or achievements in the public sphere. One woman had taken the lead in helping some of her fellow workers obtain their general equivalency diploma (GED). She proved to herself that she could act independently of her husband, and that she could do so in an effective manner. In addition, a number of women took pride in their ability to budget effectively and shop for bargains. This practical knowledge provided their families, especially the children, with opportunities they might otherwise lack. As a result of this situation, many respondents were reflectively aware of having created a personal and social identity that differed greatly from that of their mothers and grandmothers. This permitted them to cope with a variety of demands associated with everyday urban life.

Third, new social skills are important in helping women build a personal and social identity apart from that of their husbands. Working-class women must learn how to negotiate with their spouses, and they may also learn how to use impression management (Goffman 1959). They are reflectively aware of the fact that they may have to act differently at work than at home in order to cope with the tensions that develop between their husbands' more traditional expectations and the new expectations that arise at work. Therefore, some women conceal certain information about their activities in the workplace from their husbands. For example, one working-class woman had baked a cake for a party on the job, but her husband ate part of it. She had not told him what the cake was for because he would have disapproved of her "partying" at work, and she feared that he would have insisted that she quit her job.

Another pattern that emerged was that these women learned to modify their husbands' positions through effecting incremental, rather than drastic, changes. One woman indicated that she purposely makes small changes in the way she does things. Her husband "yells about it," but then he gets used to it, and then she makes other little changes. He tends to forget some of what occurred, and though he resists each change, after a time he comes to accept the reality that new expectations have arisen.

Many of these wives are aware of the need for "strategies" that will permit them to attain a greater degree of personal and social identity. They know they have not achieved the identity they aspire to, but they also realize that they have made strides in modifying their husband's actions. And most of the husbands are cognizant of the new social relationship that is emerging and begrudgingly accept many of the changes.

### Type III: A Personal and Social Identity (with Reservations)

As with the Type I working-class married women, the Type III woman, based on my interviews and fieldwork, is rare. I encountered only a few such women in my research in Austin, Corpus Christi, and Kingsville. One married woman, who was over 40, indicated that she was ready to do something different with her life. She conceded that it would be easier for her than for other women her age to make a change because she had greater financial security than other women she knew. And there were few constraints on her. She was not working and had time to think about what to do with her life.

Yet another woman in this category speaks for herself:

> I have the financial security now and I am braver. I still have more to do. I am 44, I've got money, a good car and my kids are behind me. Now, if I am not home in time to make dinner, he can make a sandwich. We've been together a long time and he knows how to make a sandwich. I have had to stand my ground. Two years ago I wanted to go to school to study for a radiologist. He didn't let me. He said I didn't have to. I got my GED. Recently ... I made a stand that I'm going out and I do. I go out during the day with friends to go out to eat. Not at night. I guess I was scared to go out. I always felt the obligation that I had to come home to cook.

These women stand apart from the typical working-class women I encountered. Because of their relative financial security, and convinced that they have played a major role in helping their husbands to achieve success, these women have developed a personal and social identity that brings them somewhat closer to the identity that college-educated women (discussed in the next chapter) take for granted.

## Resistance to Role Making

Throughout the preceding discussion, I have alluded to the husbands' resistance to the emerging social and personal identity of their wives. Working-class women recognize that their spouses often object to the fact that they are breaking away from traditional expectations. This resistance results in part from the fact that husbands do not wish to give up their traditional power and privilege (Goode 1983). But it also reflects the fact that their social power is anchored in a cultural tradition that the husbands remember and deem important. Without a social memory of their past, the husbands would be less rigid.

Still, the roadblocks to change that men construct can be exaggerated, for they are at the same time revising some of their expectations regarding their wives' actions. As the wives have been in the process of attaining a separate personal and social identity, they have been able to negotiate a new role for themselves. In Austin I discovered a small group of men who were self-critical about their roles. These men, who were members of a church group, pointed out to one another, for instance, that they should not be so overbearing with their wives, or so "macho."

The general resistance by husbands to role making is only one aspect of the problem faced by working-class Mexican American women. There is also resistance to role making by these women from the organizational structure of the community as a whole. This is a complex process, for Mexican American women are "twice a minority" (cf. Melville, 1980). Although the majority sector often assumes that it treats minorities fairly, in fact it negates them within a variety of contexts. Mexican American women are negated because of both their gender and their ethnicity. In comparison to the professional group, working-class women seem to experience greater discrimination outside the home in terms of ethnicity than in terms of gender. Although both forms of negation exist, that relating to ethnicity seems more immediate in their interaction in the larger community setting. With regard to the work world, a number of women expressed the view that Anglos "can do anything to you."

This negation—first on the basis of ethnicity and second on the basis of gender—in the public sphere makes these women highly tentative about participating in a variety of activities that are of special interest to them. For example, a number of working-class women asked me for information and assistance in dealing with the school system. They wanted to help their children, but they felt rather powerless in coping with the schools. One reason for this is a lack of confidence in their personal and social identity. In turn, this insecurity is reinforced by their fear of discrimination because of their ethnicity and gender. Their problems are compounded by their lack of knowledge about the school system and their lack of skills in serving as brokers between their children and school officials. Specifically, they lack knowledge of how to cope effectively with the forms they are expected to sign, some of which are intended more to protect the school system than to assist the children.

The resistance to role making by Mexican American women within the community seems to compel them to greater reliance on their husbands and families. This situation generates difficulties because their husbands' resistance to the creation of new roles (noted above) limits their ability to deal more effectively with community structures. Generally speaking, the patterns of discrimination within the community place constraints on role making by Mexican American working-class women in significant ways.

The activities of working-class women as twice a minority also bring other issues to light. Just how do these women cope with the contradictory role expectations regarding ethnicity and gender in the public sphere, as well as the tensions that result from their husbands' resistance to change in the familial sphere? These women cannot simply rely on the patterns of managing role tensions or conflicts outlined by Goode (1973). He speaks, for example, of the use of compartmentalization in managing role conflicts. The women use this technique to some extent; however, reality calls for them to live with what Zurcher (1986b) aptly terms a "cognitive dialectic." They must deal with contradictory role expectations—some of which are humiliating and socially painful. Many symbolic interactionists (as well as other social psychologists) downplay the contradictions that persons face in their daily lives. Yet, a number of decades ago Komarovsky (1946) analyzed the contradictory sex-role expectations for women in the privileged majority sector of U.S. society. The contradictions for minority women such as Mexican Americans are greater and have a more profound impact on the actions of these women.

## The Decision-making Process:
## Clarification of the Issues

At this juncture, we draw on our analysis of role making in examining specific decision-making areas. As suggested above, most of the research on decision making in the family has been based on "resource theory" (Blood and Wolfe 1960) and/or "exchange theory" (McDonald 1980).[4] In practice, the resource orientation implicitly employs a form of "exchange theory," and this latter orientation has come to dominate the study of decision making by husbands and wives.

The orientation of Blood and Wolfe as well as more explicit forms of exchange theory suffer from several limitations. These approaches assume that human beings are "autonomous actors" who pursue their own "self-interest" within the family. Such a view of decision making fails to take account of the fact that human beings are products of social interaction and that one's self, or identity, can never be defined totally apart from the expectations of others. Moreover, the way in which persons think is itself (as we have observed) a social process, for the "social mind" is not based, as exchange theorists assume, on some fixed biopsychological foundation.

Symbolic interactionists do not have to deny the importance of resources (the power of the paycheck, for instance), but it must be recognized that husbands and wives may interpret resources in different ways, and often resources come to be situationally defined. Although some form of exchange exists between husbands and wives, the nature of this exchange is more subtle and complex than exchange theorists recognize. To draw an analogy between exchange in the "market" and exchange between spouses ignores some fundamental realities concerning familial bonds. The relationship between spouses often involves complex forms of social and emotional dependency. The nature of social power within this context seems to be somewhat different from that in a more impersonal situation (cf. Wrong 1979).

Symbolic interactionists, unlike many exchange theorists, acknowledge that "needs" or "wants" are not fixed. They may change over time; this role making by women in particular (discussed above) is leading them to redefine their needs and wants as they attain a personal and social identity somewhat apart from that of their husbands. With this background in hand, let us proceed to an examination of certain decision-making areas.

## Specific Decision-making Areas

We shall look at five major decision-making areas. Although they do not conform neatly to those set forth by Blood and Wolfe, they do provide us with a basis for evaluating the nature of decision making within the Mexican American family.

I have used my interview data as a starting point for my analysis. Moreover, I have greatly supplemented this information with data collected through participant observation. As the research progressed, the participant observation assumed increased importance, for it provided a context within which to place some of the responses to questions in the in-depth interviews.

In general, there was considerable agreement between husbands and wives with respect to many decision-making practices. Still, some differences emerged; these are taken account of below.

*Management of Finances*

I wanted to know who is responsible for paying the bills and managing the family's income. In the interviews, I posed the general question "Who controls the finances?" and then proceeded to probe in a variety of ways regarding just what meanings are attached to this realm of decision making by both husband and wife.

Most of the couples in Austin and Corpus Christi had joint checking accounts. A few had separate accounts, and a few had no checking accounts at all. Most persons, both men and women, reported that the wife was responsible for paying the bills. Here our concern is with who pays the bills in the daily or weekly management of the family's finances. Further on, we discuss who controls the larger purchases. Who pays the grocery bills, who pays Sears, and so on?

The comments of some of the wives are revealing of the typical (or dominant) pattern.

> I pay the bills. He doesn't have the patience. He never knows what goes in and out. I do the matching and mismatching.

> I do it all. I deposit his check and mine. He doesn't know anything about the bills. But if I end up in the hospital, he can do it.

The comments of the husbands reflect those of their wives.

> She pays the bills, and she's good at that. She is more money conscious. I buy things we don't need.

> I let her pay the bills.

> She does [pay the bills]. I take her knowledge. Listen to it to arrive at a decision.

The husband who made the last comment begrudgingly admitted that he had given up control over the paying of the bills to his wife.

Although the aforementioned type of decision making is the dominant one, a relatively small group of working-class couples indicated that they assumed almost equal responsibility in taking care of weekly or monthly bills. One woman avowed, "We both take care of the finances. He reminds me, but I write the checks." Another said, "I make out the budget, but he looks at it."

Within a still smaller group of couples, the husbands paid the bills. In the words of one wife, "He does everything. I don't have to worry." And the same point was made by the husbands. Thus,

> I do everything. I pay the bills, make the checks, mail the checks. I give her the spending money she needs. . . but not because I am the man.

Just what are we to make of these observations regarding control over everyday finances? If we take the traditional husband/wife expectations as a baseline, it is clear that some changes have occurred over the past few decades. Apparently, bill paying has come to be viewed increasingly as part of the wife's "private sphere" wherein she has always had considerable influence. This has resulted in part from the fact that role making by working-class women has enabled them to acquire knowledge about the public sphere—paying bills, dealing with credit, and the like—knowledge that has permitted them to function in a somewhat independent manner.

### Purchase of a Car

"Who determines what kind of car to buy?" was another question I sought to answer. Most working-class persons, both husbands and wives, stated that the husband makes the decisions on all the criteria—model, color, and price—whether the car is for the family or for himself. Here the wives express themselves:

> He goes out o'     ˀwn to buy the truck and Mustang too. He
> gets a good de.     uys it. Then he tells me about it and I co-
> sign.

> He does. Model and color. He takes me after he picks it out.

> My husband buys it; he pays for it. He does it all.

The women rationalized their actions with the statement, "He picks out the car because I don't know too much about it." Or,

> We will go out and look at a car, and if I don't like it, he will tell me the good things about the car—for example, it doesn't use too much gas—and of course I say yes.

> He will have the final word. Most of the time I'd rather he make the big decisions. I could go out and buy a car but I don't want to. He will.

In some cases, the women did not have any say about any aspect of the car, including the color. "I didn't like the color, but the kids did." Another respondent stated,

> He said he had picked the color. I didn't like what he chose. It was brown. I didn't like it. I chose the gray and black. I had ten minutes because he had to go.

The observations of the husbands were in keeping with those of the wives. Thus,

> I bought all the cars. I bought her a little truck. I chose the color because it doesn't really matter.

> I wanted a truck and I bought it—color, model, everything. I don't ask her. If she doesn't like it, she doesn't drive it.

> I bought her a used car. She didn't want it. It had only 18,000 miles. We argued over it. She wanted a new car. We reasoned it out. We got it. Now she likes it.

There were, to be sure, exceptions to this overall pattern. In some instances, the women had an important say in selecting the color. According to one husband,

> Fuimos por el carro nuevo; fuimos para que ella escogiera el color (We went to get a new car; we went so she could choose the color).

A small subgroup of women had much greater influence over the decisions about buying a car. One of the husbands said, "I am the leader of the home, but I share my decisions in the home. I don't see why we have to fight over it. We talk." A very few women said that they had purchased their own car. Thus,

> After the last two cars, I said, hey, I'm going to pay for it. I'm
> going to choose it. It shocked him but he went along with it. I
> pay for the car from my own checking account.

As I interpret these patterns, the husband's influence in the public
sphere carries over to the purchase of a car. It has been an area of traditional male control, and on the whole the women do not view this issue as a
major one. They don't interpret the fact that the man buys the car as having
serious relevance for how they define their own power with respect to that
of their husbands.

### Responsibility for House Repairs

Decisions in this realm seem to be much in line with those relating to
the purchase of an automobile. The well-defined pattern for working-class
couples was that the husband is responsible for the house repairs.

> He does it all. He paints; he just put in new tile; and he refinished
> the cabinets. He can do just about everything.

> He is very handy. I'm not a nagging wife. He kind of oversees
> the repairs.

Some of the wives, while indicating that their husbands do the repairs
around the house, said that they have to remind their husbands about which
repairs are needed. "I tell him what needs to be done. When something
breaks, I fuss at him until he does it."

As for the husbands, almost all of them noted that they make the
repairs.

> I do them. I do the painting and put in the appliances myself. I
> did the roofing and built the shelves. I try to save money by buy-
> ing my own materials. She picked the color of the paneling.

> If I don't do them, they don't get done.

> I try to do them. Sometimes it's too costly and I try to do it.
> Takes long to do it. She's not a nagger.

In one case, the husband complained that his wife underestimated his
ability. "I put in my electric heater. And she was telling me not to leave any
wires out because of the children. I am not dumb."

Some of the husbands noted that they call on other persons to help
them with the repairs. "My neighbor across the street is very good. He helps
me."

In only a small number of instances did I encounter working-class women who insisted that both spouses were responsible for getting the house repaired. One wife spoke about the problem as follows: "He does the minor repairs around the house. However, I do the math and measuring to figure out what he needs. I get the lumber and paint and clean the yard."

Only a few persons did not do their own repairs. Concerning working-class persons, we must recognize that they have relatively modest resources, and paying for house repairs can be a costly venture. That the husbands should make the repairs is not surprising. Many of these men have during some part of their lives held jobs that required some skills as laborers. Thus, not only are they required to make house repairs through economic necessity, but they tend to have the skills necessary to carry out these tasks. And, of course, certain kinds of house repairs require considerable physical strength.

### Purchase of Furniture

Another question I asked in my in-depth interviews was, "Who decides what kind of furniture to buy?" I was interested in who makes the decisions regarding the purchase of specific items of furniture, such as a living-room suite, a bedroom suite, or a television set. I also inquired about other items of furniture, such as recliners, stereos, or videotape recorders.

Unlike the situation with respect to the purchase of a car or who makes decisions about house repairs, there is considerable diversity in the responses regarding the buying of furniture. Originally I had assumed that the women would have control over such items as the bedroom or living-room furniture and the men would most likely purchase the TV set. But the patterns were by no means as well defined as I had anticipated.

On the matter of the living-room and bedroom furniture, two main decision-making patterns emerged. One involves wives making the major decisions; the other involves a joint decision by the couples.

In one major form of decision making—that wherein the wife purchased the furniture—the women averred:

> I bought the washer and dryer. Anything I use, I buy it. It's my decision.

> I pick out the style and color. His taste is the opposite of mine.

Their husbands lent support to these statements.

> I leave it up to the women to buy that [referring to the living-room and bedroom suites].

> I let her choose; I like her taste. But I pay for it [the furniture].

In one case, the wife was consciously aware of her own role making as she engaged in the purchase of furniture.

> I like to buy furniture. I go with my daughter. I finally got this family to realize that I want to do things without asking permission.

Within the other major type — that wherein the couples saw themselves as purchasing furniture together — the wives said, "We shop together for all the furniture." The husbands supported the statements of their wives.

In only a small number of instances was the husband the main purchaser of household items. When we consider the TV set as a separate item, however, complexities arise. Few wives seem to have made the decision concerning it — either the husband alone chose the TV set or the couple did it together. Even so, some women insisted that they look for sales. Nevertheless, husbands more than wives had a major role in purchasing the TV set, "La señora se encarga de comprar (my wife is in charge of buying). She bought the living room and bedroom furniture. I like to watch TV. A mí se me puso que queria un TV (I decided I wanted a TV)."

What are we to make of this variation? During the course of my research, it became apparent that some of the traditional research regarding decision-making can be faulted because it fails to take account of the complexities of the decision-making process. The purchase of furniture illustrates several aspects of this social activity. First, husbands and wives may attach different meanings to different items in the home. Some pieces are more important to the wife, others to the husband. This situation leads to greater variation than when one is dealing with the purchase of a single item, such as an automobile.

Second, in many instances, subtle forms of negotiation seem to take place between spouses (cf. Strauss 1978). These persons cannot (and do not) take large purchases lightly, for they have limited financial resources. They thus come to an agreement through a variety of comments and discussions over time. This makes it difficult to identify the chief purchaser or decision maker concerning particular household items.

Third, some of the decisions were apparently the product of habitual action. At times, couples, when asked how they arrived at decisions, stated that they "came to an agreement" with respect to a particular purchase. I sought to probe as to the nature of this process. But some respondents simply insisted that they had "come to an agreement." In some instances I became convinced, based on the context of their comments, that this agreement had been achieved because of habitual ways of responding to each other. Couples, after living together for years, are accustomed to making decisions in particular ways. From their point of view, they make the decision together and arrive at an agreement, not through self-conscious negotiation but through habitual action (Baldwin 1988). Although the respondents were reflective about many aspects of their life, one cannot ignore the place of habit in the forming of certain decisions.

### Choice of Friends

Another area of decision making worthy of special attention is the choice of friends. I was interested in whether the wife or the husband (or both) was the chief decision maker in selecting their friends.

Two major patterns of decision making emerged. One group of couples in Austin and Corpus Christi indicated that they choose their friends on an individual basis. Another major group avowed that their friends are a product of common choice. Only a small minority of persons insisted that the husband alone determines the friendship circle.

For a number of couples, as reflected in the data from my interviews and participant observation, considerable divergence existed between the friendship circles of husbands and of wives. The wives seem to have developed women friends at work — a pattern that differs markedly from the traditional friendship patterns of women, whose friendship circles were limited to relatives or neighbors. In some instances, the husbands did not know their wives' friends. Thus, when asked who selected their friends, the wives contended:

> It varies, because I have my friends and he has his. I used to work with a lot of Chinese people, and they were my friends. He goes out with his friends at work.

> [We have] separate friends. We have work friends. We mingle but he has some and I have some and we both have some.

> I have my friends at work and I'm sure he has his. We don't socialize with a lot of people.

> I have friends at work that he doesn't know. I choose my friends. I like to go to happy hour with the girls at work, but he gets mad.

In turn the husbands responded:

> She has some friends. I have some friends at work. Friends come about through work associations.

> We each choose our friends. She talks to me about her friends
> and I talk to her about my friends. We have work friends.

> I have my friends. Work with them, drink too. She gets mad
> because I go out every Friday night with my friends. I am tired
> and I go for a few beers.

The other major kind of decision making is that wherein the husband
and wife choose at least some of their friends through mutual agreement.

> We have mutual friends. We still have friends that we had
> before we got married. We don't go out that much.

Finally, we should take account of a small subgroup of couples who do
not see themselves as having friends as such. One wife observed that her
friends live in another town. Another added, "I have a lot of relatives. But
we are loners. I am not close to my brothers and sisters." And there were
husbands who voiced a similar sentiment: "I don't have any amigos de corazón
(close friends). Maybe no más de boca (fair-weather friends) — friends are
not around when you need them." Another husband stated, "We don't have
time for friends. I don't drink. We had few friends; they're all divorced."

### Disciplining of Children

In order to uncover another dimension of decision making, I inquired
as to "Who disciplines (or punishes) the children — you or your spouse?" I
gave this problem area special attention in my field observations. In
general, the first reaction is that both husbands and wives are responsible
for the disciplining of children. But it did not take long for more subtle patterns to emerge. Two kinds of decision making appear. In the first type,
both spouses are responsible for the disciplining process, but the data suggest that the husband is much stricter than the wife. But strictness is not
equivalent to dominance. Despite the general male dominance that prevails,
women play a salient role in the disciplining of children.

In this first type, husbands and wives define themselves as sharing in
the disciplining process, but with a difference. In the second type, however,
the wife is the chief disciplinarian, although the husband is more demanding of conformity in the behavior of the children. Under the first type, the
wives made the following observations:

> My husband spanks them. I talk to them. My husband carries
> most of the weight. He is the law. Sometimes he tells the kids
> that I am too lenient. He is stricter. I discipline the children, but
> they listen to him.

I did the hollering and he did the spanking. But I was home with them.

I can scream all day and no one listens. He can say one word and they behave.

As for the husbands,

I think I do most of the disciplining, but then she does her share. Sometimes, she will say to one of the children, "I'll spank you," but she doesn't do it.

She disciplined but she was not stern. I taught them discipline and commitment. I told my wife that if they turned out right, it was because we made it happen.

We both do. I think my wife does a lot of the minor [disciplining]. For bigger things, I do it too.

In the second type, the wife is defined as the main disciplinarian; however, the husbands make their presence felt. Within this group, the wives noted:

Since I am at home, I do the disciplining. He will sometimes help, mainly with the boys. But I do it.

I never said, "We'll wait until Dad gets home," I dealt with it right then and there. [Yet]the children knew he was the head.

The husbands agreed that the wives discipline the children. "When they were little, only my wife did it." "Bueno cuando ella está ocupada me toca a mí" (Well, when she is busy, it's my job). Several added that if their wives could not control the children, they stepped in and took care of it themselves.

We don't believe in spanking unless they really deserve it. But when she needs help, she gets me to talk to them.

Again, the two groups, if taken together, reflect the typical pattern within the working class in Austin and Corpus Christi. (It also seems to be the prevailing pattern in Kingsville.) Although the groups are theoretically different, empirically they shade into each other. One group of couples stressed that they share somewhat equally in the disciplining of children but that the husband is stricter. The other group saw the wife as the main disciplinarian; however, even here the husband does some disciplining of the children and tends to be stricter.

Within both types, the wives tend to conceive of their husbands as too stern and rigid as disciplinarians, and the latter are generally aware that their wives do not always approve of this.

For example, it was not uncommon for women to say, as one mother did, "He wants to hit them. But I don't let him." Or another, "I don't intervene in front of them. A couple of times I did and this aggravated the situation." Another said, "We never agree" [over the disciplining of the children].

The husbands acknowledged this situation:

She thought I was too stern. We had fights.

My wife didn't agree with the spanking, but I had to do it.

When I spanked them, she got mad sometimes. I was strict with my son.

In practice, the wives at times intervened, directly or indirectly, in protecting the children from any harsh discipline. This seems to reflect to some degree the emerging sense of personal and social identity on the part of these women.

Some additional observations, as well as qualifications, are in order. Although the generalizations set forth above reflect the patterns I observed, certain complexities that enter into decision making regarding the disciplining of children must be recognized. A number of persons, especially husbands, recognized that their wives were the chief disciplinarians when the children were small. In addition, as children grow up, especially as they become teenagers and older, they come to influence their parents' patterns of discipline. The section on role making (see above) discussed the fact that some of the daughters encouraged their mothers to engage in this activity. More generally, in some instances "reverse socialization" comes into being. For example, one couple had reacted negatively to the behavior of their unmarried daughters, who were in their late teens and early 20s, because they had rented an apartment of their own. Nevertheless, the parents came to realize that they had to accept the actions of their daughters if they were to maintain close ties with them. Students of decision making too often overlook the fact that children may actively reshape their parents' disciplining patterns—as to both the methods and the motivations for discipline.

## Conclusions

In this chapter we turned from an analysis of changes in the extended family to a focus within the family, particularly on the interaction between working-class husbands and wives. We still take as our baseline the traditional cultural patterns when evaluating the restructuring process over the past few decades.

Certainly, working-class couples in Austin and Corpus Christi (as well as Kingsville) view their marital relationship as being very different from that of their parents. Yet they hold to rather traditional expectations regarding how wives and husbands should act. The men are to be the providers, the women the carriers of the expressive tradition, which involves taking care of the children and the home.

But these traditional expectations mask fundamental role-making processes among working-class couples, especially the women. We delineated three role-making patterns. In the most prevalent type, working-class women are striving to establish a personal and social identity somewhat apart from that of their husbands. I have emphasized that marital decision making can best be understood within the context of role making by husbands and wives. In some realms, decision making appears to be quite traditional in nature; in others, major changes seem to have occurred — the latter primarily because women are in the process of remaking their roles. When we look back at patterns within the working-class family, we discover a continual tension between tradition and change. This point becomes clearer in the analysis of changes in role making and decision making among couples in the business/professional group.

## Notes

1. It is significant that Turner did not employ the concept of role making in his major work *Family Interaction* (1970), even though he was the person who formulated the concept of role making some years earlier.

2. For more detailed information on some of the theoretical issues involved in role making, see Turner (1985). In this chapter, Turner places his own formulation within the context of modern social-psychological theory, and he discusses problems that he did not delineate in his first essay on this subject. For a theoretical and methodological evaluation of the concept of role making, see Williams (1989a).

Much work needs to be done in clarifying various theoretical and empirical issues with respect to role making. One of the areas demanding special attention is the relationship between role taking and role making. Few sociologists have grasped the significance of the basic differences between these concepts. The problems are compounded by the complex conceptual issues involved in the concept of role (Biddle 1986).

3. Most symbolic interactionists, and sociologists in general, have overlooked the fact that Mead's most influential book was *Mind, Self and Society* (1934). In fact, until recently the issue of the mind was generally ignored by sociologists.

The concept of the "social mind" is being rehabilitated in sociological theory. Randall Collins's (1989) article in *Symbolic Interaction*, and responses to it by various sociologists, will likely stimulate renewed interest in this orientation.

A number of issues regarding the social mind cannot be addressed in this book. Although I emphasize the cognitive aspects of the social mind, I realize that the social mind also encompasses emotions such as empathy that are an integral aspect of human interaction.

4. For other reviews of the vast body of literature on decision making and social power in the family, see Safilios-Rothschild (1969) and Lee (1982). Komarovsky (1988) also raises some pertinent questions regarding the study of power within the family context. A useful analysis of the power of women from a comparative perspective can be found, for example, in Dubisch (1986).

# Chapter 6    ROLE MAKING AND DECISION MAKING WITHIN THE PROFESSIONAL CLASS

In analyzing role making and decision making within the business and professional class I follow a similar format to that used in discussing these processes among the working class. I begin by examining the changing perceptions of respondents in the business and professional class (often shortened to professional) concerning how their own decision-making process differs from that of their parents. Such an approach emphasizes some major generational differences that have arisen within the Mexican American community over the past several decades. In addition, I consider the couples' sex-role expectations—ideal expectations that are not necessarily congruent with the role-making processes observed.

These data serve as a backdrop for the main issues to be addressed: role making and decision making among couples within the professional class. As we see, major differences between the working and the professional classes exist.

Here, as in the earlier chapter, my field data serve to clarify sociological issues relating to family life in general and among Mexican Americans more specifically. As this project evolved, it became apparent that the data support the view that social scientists are unable to come to terms with decision making between spouses without first considering their role-making activities.

Evidence from recent research on dual career marriages in the Anglo community indicates that role making by wives and husbands affects decision making within the conjugal family unit. For example, Hertz (1986) studied couples in which both wives and husbands occupied high-status occupations. Although Hertz does not cast her problem in these terms, spouses have been remaking their roles, and this has had a fundamental impact upon their decision making.

But I wish to make explicit what is now only implicit in the analysis of decision making and the resulting power relations between husbands and wives. This becomes all the more important when we recognize that role making as well as decision making by minorities such as Mexican Americans are shaped by the particular social circumstances of these people. Members of this group have a social memory of their traditional culture and are

110

aware of the special constraints imposed on them by their exclusion from various community and societal activities in which the majority members of society play a dominant role.

I do not elaborate only on the linkage of role making to decision making but also reexamine the use of exchange theory in interpreting decision making and social power within the family setting. We are constantly reminded of the fact that exchange theory has been the dominant theoretical framework for the analysis of this problem area. None of the subschools of thought within exchange theory seems to have fundamentally advanced our basic understanding of decision making and power relationships between spouses (cf. McDonald 1980). That is why I am advocating a highly modified form of symbolic interactionism as an alternative approach to exchange theory.

## Perceptions of Change Over Time

I wanted to know just how the couples saw their own decision-making patterns in relation to those of their parents. Just what was their perception of the changes (if any) that have occurred over time? As with the working-class couples, the respondents in the professional class, particularly during the in-depth interviews, emphasized the differences between their own conjugal relationship and that of their parents. With the exception of a few isolated individuals, they conceived of themselves as considerably less traditional than their parents. Both wives and husbands emphasized how different their marital arrangement is from that of their parents. They spoke often of the dominance of their fathers. One woman noted: "My father was negative. My mother was trapped in her situation." Other women elaborated on this theme.

> The difference is like night and day. It is a drastic change. My father was the dominant figure. He had the only voice. My mother took care of the house. When major decisions were made, he [my father] made them. I am more assertive, more firm, more willing to speak up for myself.

> My Daddy did the disciplining. He was very much in charge.

> In my house my Dad makes the decisions. My mother makes suggestions, but he's the bottom-line. He's out in the community and knows what's going on. She's a housewife. She's changed with the times.

The views of the husbands are reflected in such statements as: "My Daddy would take care of everything." Also:

> Probably with my mother, the problem was that my father did everything. Mother had to learn everything when he died. That was hard on her because she missed him too. She is doing better now.

As with the working-class persons, those in the professional class attributed the differences between their own marital relationship and that of their parents to the fact that their parents were educationally and economically deprived. According to some of the men,

> He was the only one who worked. It is quite different today — a 180-degree turn. It has to do with the times.

> It's like another century. I'm not sure it is fair to compare. Things are more available for me. Today's things were not available in the 50s.

> We are on different educational and economic levels, and that is very important. They didn't have any money.

Women provided a similar rationale for the differences. One indicated, "It's a question of economics. They [my parents] had no money, no education, and no privacy."

These reflections by respondents, both men and women, regarding their parents' situation call for elaboration. It was apparent that most of the respondents had experienced a considerable amount of upward mobility. Although a number came from the more privileged sector of the Mexican American community in Texas, others had parents who were poor. These latter understood (better than do some sociologists) that the nature of decision making among the poor is complicated by poverty. Middle-class-oriented sociologists often assume that couples have an opportunity to discuss matters with a considerable degree of privacy, without being intruded upon by children or relatives. But a number of respondents recognized that this is not the case for poor families.

We must also emphasize that although the professional respondents viewed the families in which they were reared as male dominated, they did not conclude that their fathers were totally dominant and their mothers quiet, weak, and submissive. In most instances, they saw their mothers as playing some role in the decision-making process. Contrary to the stereotypes that continue to be advanced by some social scientists, Mexican

American women, even some decades ago, exerted a measure of control, at least in the private sphere.

Furthermore, a minority of the respondents emphasized the strength of the mother's role within the family of orientation.

> In my house my father worked out of town. My mother had to run everything, the discipline, all the decisions.

> My mother did it all. Spanking too. My mother was very dominant, yet my father did the grocery shopping, paid bills, etc. She was smart. She made him believe that he was in control. She made him think that it was his idea. She was very domineering that way.

> My mother was active in the PTA and helped with political campaigns. She also took care of the finances. My father gave her the money and she managed the money for the family.

My observations suggest that the Mexican America professionals from more economically advantaged families credited their mothers with more influence than did those from more disadvantaged backgrounds. But even many of the latter recognized that the influence of their mothers was not to be discounted.

### Sex-role Expectations

On the matter of the definition of their own and their spouses' role expectations, the dominant pattern in both Austin and Corpus Christi was conformation to the traditional ideal of the husband as provider and wife as the carrier, in Parsons's terminology, of the expressive side of family life (Parsons and Bales 1955).

The professional women saw themselves as taking care of the home and children and as providing the husband with social and emotional support. The men, though recognizing that they had a role to play as fathers, viewed themselves primarily as the chief financial supporters and the representatives of the family in the broader community. Some professional women observed:

> I make sure that they [the children] have everything they need — clothes, food, being taken places. He's always busy.

> I provide the home life — see things are in order, pay the bills. He's so busy.I have to assume a lot [of the responsibility at home].

> The most important thing my husband is supposed to do is to be a provider and maintain a happy marriage and family life. He should support us financially and morally and provide stability and security. He should provide guidance. I see him more as an authority figure, not as having the upper hand.

The husbands expressed themselves as follows concerning the wife's role:

> She should take care of the family—be a perfect mama. She should make us happy by maintaining an atmosphere whereby our children and I can grow and develop.

> In my opinion, take care of me.

> Be a mother to my children.

> She should take care of the household. She should take care of the kids, pay the bills, etc. In general, we have a modern household. She is very busy with kids. Just car pooling takes a lot of time.

The husbands' perceptions of their own roles generally mirrored those of their wives. For instance,

> My job is to be a provider, husband and father. I need to make sure that my son gets what he wants and needs. To a large degree, our kids come first in our lives. I provide shelter and security and opportunity for growth.

While the aforementioned role expectations were the dominant ones expressed, two subtypes emerge within the professional class that are not apparent in the working class. In one subtype, the respondents, when discussing their own and their spouses' expectations, reported that providing support and communication between husband and wife is an essential aspect of sex-role expectations. One woman observed that "communication is very important. Sex is very important. We like to talk to each other. I know exactly what he is thinking." Several wives mentioned the significance of communication not only with their husbands but also with their children. "It is important to listen to the children."

The husbands within this subtype spoke about being supportive and regarded talking and sharing experiences with one's spouse as an integral part of marriage. "Sometimes we just want to talk, to take an interest in what we are sharing." Moreover, "I try to get the kids to recognize that I am also their friend. And I let them grow so they do not get frustrated and develop paranoia."

Still another subtype, though it includes few persons, merits attention because these couples show an even sharper break from traditional role expectations in that husband and wife function within separate spheres. This new orientation came to light particularly in the statements of some of the men in the professional class.

> I do the same thing she does. Traditionally, the husband had to be the breadwinner. In our family, we have two breadwinners, two homemakers.

> I don't mind admitting that my wife helps me to bring in the money. It gives us a better standard of living.

Also,

> Oh my God, I've changed my way of living so much. Now we are equal. If she cooks, I will wash the dishes. Or if I cook, she will do the dishes. She earns as much as I do. I help her a lot. I do more around the house than she does. I don't know if she will agree with this or not.

The views of the wives belonging to this subtype are well expressed in the statement of one professional woman:

> My role is to be a good role model. I am very honest with my family, for I attempt to teach them about current issues and answers. I do not see myself as a person who cooks and cleans. I am an equal worker. The husband's main function is giving a bit of himself to all of us.

This break from traditional sex-role expectations by a minority of the professional class is reflected to an even greater degree in actual practice when we look closely at the role-making process, especially by the women.

### The Role-making Process

While the wives in the working and professional classes are alike in that they, rather than their husbands, are taking the lead in creating new roles for themselves, the differences between the women in these two sectors are striking. The professional women, even the most traditional among them, had already achieved a personal and social identity that working-class women were still struggling to construct.

The professional women, after all, had attended college (the great majority of them had at least one college degree). Their achievements in the educational realm had led to, as well as reinforced, a sense of social identity that set them somewhat apart from that of their fathers and husbands. Later success in the occupational sphere, or in other public endeavors, had provided them with a self-justification for sustaining this identity. Their skills and knowledge made it possible and feasible for them to participate in the public sphere in ways that were not available to traditional Mexican American women such as their mothers and grandmothers. Their educational and occupational background also permitted a greater variety of responses to role making than was found among the working class.

Among the professional couples, only a few (five among those I formally interviewed, all of them living in Austin) were seeking to create roles for themselves that called for equality within the conjugal relationship. This ideal of equality was not expressed by any working-class couple. Although the professional couples were few in number, and in practice had not achieved the equality ideal, they nonetheless had broken from traditional expectations. A few were in their 20s, a few in their 40s. Among the latter, the struggle for equality resulted from personal crises in the family (such as the husband's disability) that forced the wife to assume many duties associated with the husband's role, such as becoming the primary breadwinner. These women recognized that their husbands' identity was threatened thereby, a fact confirmed by the men.

For theoretical reasons, I have singled out the few couples who are striving to attain an egalitarian ideal. At the least, their small number raises serious questions about research that assumes equality between Mexican American spouses (Cromwell and Cromwell 1978; and Ybarra 1977, 1982). These data also help to place the role-making (as well as decision-making) patterns described below within a broader perspective.

On the basis of the data obtained from in-depth interviews and participant observation, four kinds of role making emerge. These types are constructed primarily on the basis of two interrelated criteria: One concerns the authority patterns between husbands and wives, and the other the relative emphasis that women give to duties at home in contrast to those in the public sphere, primarily the workplace. (The small number of women who were not employed at the time of the research were all involved in community activities and thus were active participants in the public sphere.) Here we are emphasizing the perspective of the women because they are taking the lead in remaking their relationships with their husbands.

### Type I. The Reluctant Dependent

Only a small group of women (four, and perhaps one other, of those I formally interviewed) fall into this category, but so do several wives I talked with in the course of my participant observation. All these women were working outside the home.

These professional women had already achieved the identity that the working-class women typically were striving to attain. Their self-recognition of autonomy is captured by one woman: "If we ever divorced, I know I can support myself and my children." Although she (and others) were confident of their ability to function in the public sphere, they still deferred to their husbands and were heavily dependent on them for their sense of self-worth.

This type of professional woman accepts the fact that the husband can and does structure her life. The husband is the authority figure in the home and delegates the tasks for his wife to carry out. He also insists that she be at home with the children in the evening, and he does not approve of her carrying out tasks related to her job after work. "He feels resentment when I bring work home. He tells me I should spend more time with him. He gets mad [when I don't do so]."

These women are insecure, and one way this is expressed is in their jealousy and concern with their husbands' whereabouts. According to one woman, "He knows how to trigger it. Maybe it's his ego. It makes him feel good. What man wouldn't like it, for his wife to be jealous?" Yet this same woman expressed serious personal reservations about her own reactions.

The constraints imposed by the husband carry over into the wife's work world. These women are generally unhappy with their jobs, but they find it difficult to change their occupations because they need the approval of their spouses. In one instance, the husband insisted that his wife continue in her occupation because he found it in his economic interest to do so. Another woman wanted to change jobs, but her husband did not support her in this action; she remained in the same position. Moreover, because the husbands restricted their wives' friendship circles, the women found it difficult to gain the support of significant others for actions they wanted to carry out.

The husbands of some of these women were the only men I encountered who overtly appealed to traditional Mexican American cultural traditions to justify their place of authority within the family. Although those who openly espoused this view were few in number, the pattern does illustrate the way in which social memory of traditional expectations can affect authority relations within the family. (The role of the memory of traditional expectations in other men's actions toward their wives was less apparent.)

Contradictions exist in these more traditional husbands' expectations regarding the wife's role. For husbands of Type I women, this subtype (including those who openly spoke of sustaining traditional expectations) not only wanted but also expected their wives to work outside the home. They depended on their spouses' incomes to sustain their standard of living and advance their aspirations for upward mobility in the educational and the occupational spheres.

The wives seem to have accepted their situation because of insecurities associated with their own life histories. All the women in this subtype experienced traumatic childhoods (more so than women in the other subtypes); thus they interpreted their marriage as a major source of stability, even when they voiced serious reservations to me regarding their actions and their husbands' definition of their role.

### Type II. Semi-independent, Family Oriented

The majority of the business/professional women fall into this category. Typically, it includes the wives (and their husbands) who articulate the egalitarian ideal. In addition, this group subsumes those women who were not working at the time of the research but who were active in a variety of community activities outside the home.

As these women define their situations, the family takes precedence over public activities, including their careers. Yet they have a more well-defined sense of their own personal worth than do the Type I women, and they are not as dependent on their husbands. They often recognize their own independence by contrasting their lives with those of their mothers. A number of women observed that "my mother never worked," and they were aware that this limited their mothers' power and authority within the family. Today, as in the past, the relationship between husband and wife is to some degree bound up with the question of who has control over financial decisions that move beyond the private realm.

The roles carried out by these professional women have certain built-in contradictions. In particular, the women employed outside the home—and they constituted the bulk of the women studied—were engaged in a struggle to maintain their identity as career women, along with their identity as wives and mothers. "My responsibility is to my daughter and the home. I feel I need to be home. That's why I don't go out to happy hour"—though it would have been advantageous to her career for this woman to do so. Another commented, "I love my kids. That's why I work. The [economic] help I provide is for them." Thus the commitment to a career is often justified on the grounds that it provides greater opportunities not just for themselves but also for their children.

In general, the women gain from their careers considerable personal and social satisfaction, including a rather strong sense of personal and social identity. At the same time, their work outside the home is not an end in itself, for it provides the family, especially the children, with social and educational opportunities that they would not otherwise have. In a basic sense, these women want to be supportive wives and caring mothers. One way of minimizing the role strain between the demands of the job and the demands of being a wife and mother is to "compartmentalize" their lives and give priority to motherhood over their careers.

The women fulfill their commitment as mothers in a variety of ways. For example, they carefully screen their children's day-care centers and are attentive to their children's progress in school. It is the wives, not the husbands, who intervene with day-care personnel and teachers at school on behalf of their children. The tensions for these women, however, are intensified during periods of crisis such as a child's illness. The respondents expressed guilt about the paucity of time they spent with their children.

> The home environment pace has to be set by the woman. I work long hours and different shifts. It's hard on the family. My boys had to learn to be independent. It's all worked out anyway. I have good kids.

Another woman commented that her children are still young and that she feels guilty about leaving them all day. While she wants to be successful in her career and knows that she can be, the tensions that arise are difficult to manage. This kind of situation is very frustrating, and she views herself as struggling more with motherhood than with her career. A number of these women pointedly expressed regret over the frequent need to spend time in work related activities after 5:00 P.M.

Because the ideal expectations clash with the demands of work, these women have had to engage in creative role-making activities. They cannot deal with this situation through compartmentalizing their worlds—saying to themselves that they will spend so much time with their children and so much time at work. Thus they seek to carry out particular activities that serve to symbolize a commitment to being a good wife and mother. One woman said, "I will make time to bake for them. My husband tells me not to do it, but I feel I have to." Why this symbolic action? Through it, the woman "justifies" to herself that she is a good mother and rationalizes away the time spent outside the home.

A number of Type II women also seem to distinguish between their role as wife and their role as mother. They go out of their way to maintain communication with their husbands, something the Type I women did not mention. "Our lives have changed because we both have heavy loads at our job, and we have to help each other." In this context, helping means providing emotional support for each other's activities. Tensions arise because of the lack of time and financial resources for these couples to be alone with each other, even during vacations.

The husbands' expectations of their wives' role correspond to those of the wives. The husbands expect their wives to care for the home and children, and they assume this arrangement to be the proper one. Although a few husbands assist with the housework and child care, they define these duties as the primary responsibility of their wives, who in turn complain about the situation.

> It's unfair. Women have to do things that they are expected to do. Hold on to housekeeping responsibilities. We are Supermoms. I teach, and as a mother, I work all night.

These women learn to live with certain levels of built-in tension as a result of the "Supermom" expectations. They come tacitly to accept the fact that "cognitive dissonance" inheres in their role. But for all the accommodations they make, they still cannot rid themselves of the dialectic tensions that exist (Zurcher 1986b). The idea of the dialectic is that there is an ongoing process of accommodation to the tensions that arise in diverse social situations.

### Type III. Semi-independent, Career Oriented

These women constitute the second largest group. They are far more committed to their careers than Type II women, and they speak about advancing themselves in the business and professional spheres. A number are intent on continuing their education in order to achieve their occupational goals. They are less committed to being homemakers than Type II women: they are also less committed to this than are Type I women. Nevertheless, they take child care seriously and experience strains between being a mother and being a career woman. Several women broke down and cried when they spoke about the demands of their career often taking precedence over motherhood.

In general, the husband of a Type III woman does not want to give up his power as controller of the family's finances. Nevertheless, he says he supports his wife's career. Several husbands captured the ambivalence of men married to Type III women when they tacitly admitted that their wives were more skilled in their work than they were in their own.

Although Type III women gain a strong sense of personal and social identity from their work, they nevertheless define their husbands' careers as more significant, in financial terms, than their own. Thus, one woman asked for a job transfer in order to open up a position for her husband. In addition, several husbands married to this type of woman were quick to observe that they made more money than their wives. Although the wives' commitment to their careers did to some extent undermine the husbands' authority, and the husbands resisted the relinquishing of authority, they were not willing to give up the social and economic advantages that accrued from the additional family income. Ultimately, these husbands have given up some of their traditional authority.

### Type IV. Independent, with Constraints

This kind of role-making pattern among married Mexican American women is uncommon. Only two women whom I interviewed belong to this type, although I met several others like them during the course of my participant observation.

The Type IV woman conceives of her career as being more important than her husband; however, she has not achieved equality in her conjugal relationship. Typically, the husband is disadvantaged (educationally or in some other respect) in comparison to his wife. The role strain experienced by this type of woman is quite different from that among women in the other subtypes. This woman is engaged in a role-making pattern in which she minimizes her own importance in the conjugal relationship. For example, one woman was careful in the home not to make too much of her career or her monetary success because her husband felt threatened by her achievements. He conceded that it was difficult for him to accept his wife's role as a successful career person and the chief wage earner. Another wife commented:

> I started to work and get involved with civic issues. His pride began to show, and we started to argue. I guess he was jealous because I really enjoy my work. It wasn't easy for me, and I don't want you to think that it was.

She was consciously reshaping her role to minimize conflict with her husband and the threat to his identity, for she (like other women in this group) valued her marital status very highly.

### Constraints on Role Making

When considering the nature of role making within the family, we must keep in mind that these changes occur within the context of larger community and organizational contexts (McCall and Simmons 1982). The family does not exist in social vacuum.

When we examine role making patterns by husbands and wives within the larger organizational and community setting, we first of all perceive some differences between Austin and Corpus Christi. Austin, as the seat of the state capitol and the University of Texas, and during the 1980s the center of an emerging computer industry, has offered greater opportunities for economic advancement, especially for women, than has Corpus Christi. Even so, Austin is not a locus of large corporate headquarters, and thus certain kinds of opportunities associated with climbing the corporate ladder (cf. Hertz 1986) are unavailable in Austin (in contrast to, for example, Los Angeles, which includes a large Mexican American population). Still, if one compares Austin and Corpus Christi to a smaller community such as Kingsville, the similarities are more striking than the differences.

Nevertheless, the relative lack of economic opportunity in Corpus Christi seems rather directly related to role making by certain professional women. A number of them commented to me that they wanted to advance in their careers but that to do so would mean leaving the city, and this would likely lead to ruptures in their family arrangements.

But we must examine the problem of social and economic opportunities within a broader framework. This is especially true when we consider Mexican American women (who are taking the lead in the role-making process) as "twice a minority." Like their working-class counterparts, they face constraints imposed by both their gender and their ethnicity. Yet the manner in which these constraints affect role making by professional women differs somewhat from that within the working class.

In general, professional women, more so than working-class women, are keenly aware of the constraints imposed on them by gender and ethnicity. Working-class women conceive of ethnicity as a more compelling issue than gender; professional women typically perceive gender issues as more salient than ethnicity. Thus, negation in terms of gender on the job and in the community seems to be relatively greater for professional than for working-class women.

As women move up the occupational ladder, the co-workers they encounter are those who have become somewhat more guarded with respect to negation on the basis of ethnicity. This is not as true in the case of gender. Overly negative reactions toward gender seem to be somewhat more acceptable as a means of social control than overt negation based on ethnicity. This is not to say that ethnic discrimination can be ignored, and these women are attuned to the subtle forms it takes. What makes the situation complicated for Mexican American women is that the manner in which gender and ethnicity interact varies considerably from one social situation to the next. In addition, many of the respondents commented on how difficult it is for them to separate negation in terms of gender from negation based on ethnicity.

Certainly negation in terms of ethnicity cannot be ignored, for women as well as for men. Looking back over my field notes, I can point to a number of social gatherings during which the issue of negation based on ethnicity was a major topic of conversation by both sexes. One social event in Austin stands out in this respect, for discussion throughout the evening focused on the problems various Mexican Americans had encountered as a result of their ethnicity—and the various ways in which they had been "put down" by majority members of society.

The constraints upon role making experienced by professional women in the public sphere serve, as they do for working-class women, to inhibit role making in the private sphere of the family. A number of the respondents, because they lacked the needed support within the broader community and organizational context, found it almost impossible to engage in Type IV role making. The family remained their major source of support.

As for Mexican American professional men, they have, except for the husbands of women engaged in Type I role making, made important adaptations and changes. Many men in their late 30s and 40s commented on how dramatically they had changed during the course of their marriage. Their perceptions of how much they differ from their fathers and grandfathers are very real. Yet there is also evidence that role changes by professional men are less apparent in the public than in the private sphere. In the public realm they have sustained a more traditional view of their male role with respect to women—though some role making has been taking place. The men, as they function in the community and organizational spheres, receive considerable support, even from Anglo men, for traditional role expectations.

### The Decision-making Process

As in the preceding chapter, we are here concerned about decision making with respect to the management of finances, purchase of a car, responsibility for home repairs, purchase of furniture, choice of friends, size of family, and disciplining of children. We are intent on presenting data that explicate the patterns regarding decision making between husbands and wives within the professional class; these patterns are in some respect similar to, and in other respects rather different from, those in the working class. In addition, we are seeking to open up new ways of understanding how and why husbands and wives come to make decisions affecting the family.

Decision-making theory has relied heavily on "resource theory," one form of exchange theory. In fact, as Rubin (1976:175) sees it, the two can perhaps be equated:

Simply stated, resource theory conceptualizes marriage as a set of exchange relations in which the balance of power will be on the side of the partner who contributes the greater resources to the marriage. While not made explicit, the underlying assumption of this theory is that the material contributions of the husband are the "greater resource."

Resources are important in decision making, but it is through the interaction of husbands and wives that the nature of what is a "resource" comes to be defined. The data support the thesis that role making is an important foundation stone for understanding decision making. One cannot seriously consider decision making in a rapidly changing social order without first grasping role making. Moreover, the complex emotional involvements of husbands and wives, and the interdependency that emerges over time, lead to decisions that cannot be equated with impersonal decisions in an economic market, as in auctions (which social scientists often use to illustrate the ideal type of economic exchange where the law of supply and demand is seen in rather stark terms—see Thurow 1983). Again, exchange theory, especially that based on the "economic man," depersonalizes the social relations associated with most family interaction.

### Management of Finances

Our main concern has been with understanding which spouse in the marriage relationship manages and controls the finances. There is greater variability in decision making in the professional than in the working class, a pattern made possible by the professional class's greater financial and educational resources.

The dominant subtype is that wherein the couples pool their income and the wife decides which bills need to be paid during the course of the week or the month. Some of the responses of the spouses clarify this pattern. First the wives:

> I do the budget, take care of the bank account. I write the checks and pay the bills. I handle all the finances.

> He would worry to find out how much money goes out to all the bills.

> I wanted to do it. I have more time with the kids now that they are grown up. He used to make it so hard and it's easy.

Next the husbands:

> She pays all the bills, does the budget-the whole bit. She keeps me informed.

> I used to do it until three years ago. She wanted to take over.

> I have been forcing it on her in the last three years. She needs to know how to spend money paying bills. I think it's important for her to know.

Though there is discussion of finances, the wife pays the bills. She makes the primary decisions in the weekly and monthly budgeting of their common income.

Another subtype, not as large as the first, is that in which the husband pays the bills (this pattern seems to be more prevalent in Corpus Christi than in Austin). Here the reflections of the husbands articulate the issues even more effectively than do the comments of their wives.

> She wants me to do it right now.

> When we first got married, I did it. When she stayed home with the baby, she did it. I thought she needed to do it. Now that she is working, I do it again.

> I hate it. Neither of us likes to do it. I just do it because someone has to.

The wives in this group do not appear to perceive the husband's role in this area as a threat to their power; that is, they do not define themselves as dependent simply because their husbands pay the bills. Instead, managing the finances tends to be viewed as a distasteful task that must be done by someone. By their own admission, the women in this group want their husbands to assume this responsibility.

Finally, there is a small subtype in Austin, but not in Corpus Christi, in which the couples are moving toward a sharing of responsibility in managing the finances; at least they strive for this ideal. One woman said, "Sometimes I do it, and sometimes he does it. When we were younger, he did it all. But I feel that it is an equal thing and we should both be on top of it." A few other couples were developing a relationship in which each spouse is responsible for paying half the bills.

One wife clearly set forth this decision-making process, and her husband concurred in her statements.

> We have separate checking accounts. I take care of my own car payment, the house payment, my own credit cards, and clothes for the kids. He takes care of the utilities, life insurance, his own credit cards, the groceries, and so on. At one time, he took care

of all the bills. I was unhappy because I did not feel I had a say.
He was frustrated because he had a lot of responsibilities. The
idea of separate accounts works well.

It is apparent that this last-mentioned subtype has no counterpart among
the working-class couples and reflects an effort to sustain equality in the
financial arena.

As I reexamined the comments of my respondents, I found that some
couples exhibited certain changes over time in their management of
household finances. In some instances, the changes in decision making
resulted from newly emerging life circumstances, such as children growing
up and leaving home. In other instances, they occurred because both wives
and husbands were engaged in remaking their roles. This shifting nature of
decision making resulting from role making cannot be ignored.

It is only recently that symbolic interactionists have become explicitly
aware of the factor of "time" (cf. Denzin 1987) when seeking to unravel the
multidimensional, and at times contradictory, nature of human interaction. As couples move through their life course, decision making comes to
be restructured, a phenomenon that has typically been brushed aside by
sociologists who have analyzed decision making within this framework.

### Purchase of a Car

Various probing questions during in-depth interviews sought to uncover who determines the car's model, color, and accessories. Also, I inquired as to who was going to drive the vehicle. My original assumption was
that the person who decides on the model of the car, especially, is the one
who wields the greater power in the family. But this turned out to be too
simple an assessment.

Inasmuch as the professional couples owned more than one car and inasmuch as they purchased cars more frequently than the working-class
couples, the questions regarding the purchase of an automobile assumed
somewhat greater meaning for them than for working-class couples.

One subtype (about half of the interviewees) perceived the husband as
the primary decision maker with respect to the kind of car selected.
Significantly, the men attached greater meaning to the model of the car
than did the women.

Among the wives, observations such as the following were typical:

The Camaro sitting outside was chosen by him. He signed the
contract and bought the car.

His ideas prevail over mine. He tries to persuade me. He thinks
I'm negative.

A few wives indicated that the husband bought the car for their birthday or for Mother's Day. "It was a surprise. I had said I liked an LTD and he bought it for me."

The husbands responded:

> The decision to buy the car is mine. I choose the size of the motor and the radials. I know more about cars [than she does]. She lets me make the total decision on the car.

> I choose one model but she wants a certain color and it usually is not available.

> I do the legwork. I choose the model. She [my wife] shares in the final decision. I'm the one who knows about cars. She could care less.

> I'll be probably the first one to look. After that, we'll look at it. I guess I'm the one to pick it out. The choice of color is probably hers.

Within this group (where the husbands made the key decisions regarding the car), a number mentioned that the wives chose the color of the car. As one woman noted, "I have the say on the color, and he picks out the air conditioner for me."

Several other subtypes of decision making emerged. In one of these (found only in Austin), each spouse made all the decisions on his or her car. A typical response of the wives was: "I chose my car — both the model and the color. I've always wanted a big car, and I bought what I wanted." And, "If I hadn't liked it, we would not have bought it." The men in this group echoed this view. "I determine the kind of car I want and she picks her own car. She chooses everything for her car." Or, "I bought a car without telling her, and she bought a car without telling me."

In still another subtype, which included only a few couples, the spouses bought the car jointly. One wife reported, "We went to see the cars, and we decided which one we wanted." In some cases, the wife's part in the joint decision was that of the husband. "He [my husband] tends to be more extravagant. I tend to be very practical. I don't like accessories, we don't need them. I want it to be useful." One of the husbands within this group commented that he shops for a car first and then informs his wife what he wants to buy. He waits for her indication that they should move forward on the matter, for he admitted he has a tendency to be an impulsive buyer. In addition, the husband reported that he does not make decisions on big items without his wife's approval because if it turns out to be a mistake, he does not want to be blamed.

In general, the professional men still play a significant role in purchasing the car, but the wives in this group wield greater influence than do those in the working class. Moreover, the professional couples exhibit considerable diversity in the manner in which they make decisions in this area.

### Responsibility for House Repairs

Among professional couples, the decisions in this sphere are made by the husbands. They are responsible for repairs to leaky faucets or the garbage disposal.

The wives indicated that "the husband usually does them [house repairs]. That is his role as husband and a father." Or, "He knows more about the house. He does everything, he paints, does the yard, and so on". Yet most men were not experts in fixing more complex items such as the electrical system, and here specialists were called in.

The husbands' responses supported these generalizations.

> I'll look at it and, if I think I can do it, I'll fix it. I fix the faucets, paint the house, take care of the yard. If I cannot fix it myself, only then will I call, for example, the plumber.

> I do it. Too expensive to have someone do it.

There are, as one might expect, some variations on the role of husbands in making house repairs. One subtheme is reflected in the statement: "I am responsible for the house repairs, but if the washing machine breaks down, it is her responsibility to call the repairman to have it fixed." In some instances, when household equipment used by the wife breaks down, she is expected to take the lead in getting it repaired.

In a small subgroup of couples, the women viewed themselves as having equal responsibility for taking care of the repairs. "I come from a family of fix-it-alls. I do it." Or, "I usually call the plumber or whoever to come fix it." Several women saw themselves as sharing the responsibility, for either they bought the materials their husbands used or they helped them make the repairs.

Nevertheless, it is clear that the husbands in the professional class were the dominant decision makers with respect to house repairs; this is one arena in which the traditional role expectations are reflected more clearly in the decision-making activities in everyday life.

### Purchase of Furniture

As with the working-class couples, the purchase of furniture by the professional couples poses special difficulties for the analysis of decision making. Couples are called on to choose among multiple items, and they interpret the importance of these in differing ways in the context of interaction patterns that are not always easy for the participants to articulate. For some, furniture-buying decisions were situationally determined, and further, some couples disagreed somewhat over which spouse had made a particular decision and over how it was reached. (Closed-ended questionnaires cannot adequately capture the vagaries of decision making as it occurs over time.)

The two major subtypes of decision making are those in which (l) the wife selects the bedroom and living-room furniture and the husband buys the TV set; and (2) husband and wife purchase furniture together (including the TV set). As to the former, the following responses by husbands reflect the patterns that emerged.

> I let her select the living-room furniture. I really don't care about it. The stereo was my idea.

> I would buy the videotape recorder because I have expertise in electronics. We buy the things that are in our area of expertise.

In the second major subtype, where the couples purchase furniture together, a common response follows Strauss's (1978) idea of negotiated order. "We compromise. We go together and see several pieces and decide on one." My own field observations suggest that when both spouses shop together, the decisions are the result of negotiations as to what each person likes and how much they can afford to spend. But the matter is more complex than this. After couples live together for some years, they apparently reach understandings about each other's needs and orientations, and they therefore often arrive at decisions through indirect means. They have established taken-for-granted assumptions (Garfinkel 1967) that do not require the "formal negotiations" that are typical of more impersonal relationships. I mentioned in the previous chapter — and reiterate here — that habit also seems to come into play in certain decisions made by couples.

In another subtype (which includes fewer persons than those above), the husbands purchased all the furniture. According to one wife,

> He shops more than I do. He decided that we needed a new bed and I agreed. He bought the living-room furniture too. He buys the TV. He watches it; I don't like it.

This statement finds support in the comments of some husbands.

> I'm the one that instigates the buying. I bought the couch. I bought the bed and the TV. I would buy the videotape recorder, but I don't want one. I see good buys and get them.

We talked about it and I surprised her with the TV. But it is not
a male thing with me. I bought her a dishwasher because the old
one broke. [She kept complaining about it, so I got one.]

In still another, rather small subgroup, the women bought all the furniture. One woman observed, "He was in shock when I bought the TV."
From another woman: "Usually I try to get a head start on it. I go look at
the style and price. Then I tell him about it. I do most of the shopping. I
have more time." In this instance, the woman takes the lead, but keeps the
husband informed of what is happening. The views of the husbands who
went along with this orientation are: "I leave it up to her. I usually like what
she buys."

These data underscore the fact that the wives in the professional class
exert more power or influence than do their working-class counterparts.
Then, too, the professional couples have broken markedly from the traditional expectations of the past, in that women seem to have a greater say.
As to equality, the patterns are not easy to assess. My field observations
suggest that the men still are somewhat more dominant than the responses
suggest. Even so, the purchase of, for example, a TV set or other electronic
items (which may signify greater control by males in the public sphere) is
not defined as a major issue by some of these women. And many of the professional women now participate directly or indirectly in decision making
on these items.

### Choice of Friends

When we examine how professional couples select their friends, we
must keep the traditional patterns in mind. Grebler et al. (1970:353) state
that "in the traditional extended kin group, visiting is especially important
for women. For them it is often the major form of recreation, and it tends
to be confined to relatives, even to the exclusion of neighbors." Although
these authors recognize that, with urbanization and acculturation, these
patterns have undergone considerable modification, they do not specify the
manner in which their choice of friends has evolved.

Typically, the wife's occupational status has played a major role in the
creation of the couple's friendship network. The dominant pattern is that
the husband and wife have mutual friends, but, in addition, both have some
friends of their own.

As the women state:

I choose my own friends. Some are work friends. They are
teachers and we go out together as couples.

> I have friends at work and he has friends at the office. He travels a lot on his job. Our staff is mostly Chicanos, so a lot of my friends are Chicanos — mostly men. His friends are mostly women. He works with a lot of women.

> He has a lot of friends at work that I don't know, and I know friends that he doesn't know at work.

> At first all of our friends were his. For a long time I wouldn't mix with my friends at work. That's changed.

The men support this general conception of the choice of friends.

> We both have mutual friends. But I have some friends through my job and she does too. Also, she has friends in a women's organization.

> I have my friends at work and she has hers at work. We try to get together but it doesn't work out. Her friends are older than we are. Most of mine are single; it doesn't work out to bring them home.

Another variant on this theme is: "She has her own friends — at church and in connection with her work in the arts. I came to know my friends through my work, and some are in the reserves."

These responses regarding friendship patterns become more understandable if we realize that when both spouses work, husband and wife often are too busy to socialize except on the job or in certain community activities (cf. Lawe and Lawe 1980). For some of the husbands and wives, friendship ties at work are important in supporting their respective careers. Also, many of the respondents invest considerable time and effort in a variety of community activities. For example, as mothers, many women feel obligated to spend time participating in their children's activities, from Girl Scout meetings to Little League baseball games.

The constraints of time imposed by work and community activities shape the women's (and men's) friendship network. One woman said: "We don't entertain much. We have lunch with friends. We go to meetings and see friends; we like to socialize with them at meetings." That both partners are extremely busy is also noted by many of the husbands. "We don't really have the time to go out and socialize with friends. But when we do, I guess it is fifty-fifty. She meets her friends and I meet mine."

In addition to the dominant pattern regarding choice of friends, two other subtypes emerged. One is where the husband selects the couple's friends, a pattern that holds most clearly for the Type I role making, discussed earlier. But some of the husbands of women who fall into the other role-making types also took the lead in the selection of friends (more often in Corpus Christi than in Austin). One husband's remarks are typical. "Most of the friends that we see are from contacts that I have initiated." In another subgroup, the wife was primarily responsible for selecting the couple's friends. According to the husbands, "It is not that she chooses them, but that she has more opportunity to meet people. We get invited to functions that involve her friends from work." With another couple, the wife conceded that she chooses their friends because she is a jealous person. "I don't let him be himself. I choose all our friends."

And then there is a small handful of couples who lack friends in the community. They attributed this to the fact that they do not have relatives in town, and they therefore stay at home. One wife viewed her husband as a quiet person who does not enjoy socializing.

Even taking account of various exceptions, it is apparent that most couples have established a friendship network independently of the family setting—a fact confirmed by both my interviews and my participant observation.

### Disciplining of Children

There were more disagreements between husbands and wives regarding the disciplining of children than in any other area. Some of the lack of agreement was over who is the primary decision maker, but most of it centered on how the children should be disciplined.

There are two main subtypes of couples. In one the husband is seen as the chief disciplinarian or the disciplinarian of last resort. In the other the husband and wife share more or less equally in this task. Then there is a third subtype (smaller in size) wherein the wife is seen as the chief disciplinarian; more mothers than fathers view themselves in this light. In the subgroup that sees the husband as the main disciplinarian, the wives made observations such as "I did it [the disciplining] but he spanked them." But not all husbands viewed as the chief disciplinarian (or the disciplinarian of last resort) spank children as a way of controlling them.

He talks a lot about what he expects out of them. He's a calm person.

His thing is to send them to their room, and he won't let them out until it's over. He seldom spanks.

The husbands in this group tended to complain that their wives are not strict enough with the children.

> She says she does [the disciplining], but I do it. I am the last resort.

> She will let them know how angry she is, but ultimately I punish the children.

> I was more rigid, more traditional, more strict. She did it but wasn't firm enough.

> I do [the disciplining]. I take most of the responsibility. But I'm sure she does it when I am not at home.

The last comment is worth emphasizing, for it makes the point that, even where the husbands claim major responsibility for disciplining the children, a number of them are aware that their wives carry out this function when they are not around.

Another group of couples insisted that they share rather equally in punishing the children for misbehavior. One father's statement captures the pattern expressed by several others: "When the children were growing up, we both did it. But when she did it, I stayed out of it; and when I did it, she stayed out of it." Another expressed himself as follows: "I use a stern voice to teach them discipline. My wife does it the old-fashioned way of slapping their butt."

The women in this group made observations such as:

> He disciplines in a quiet way. I am big on yelling. Both of us handle it, even when they were little. I was never the type to say, "Wait until your father gets home." I took care of it when it was needed. But we always felt that we had to do it together.

> We both do. Sometimes we disagree. I do more spanking.

Within the smaller subgroup in which the wife was seen as the chief disciplinarian, some women said:

> My husband is weaker than I am. He feels guilty because he does not spend that much time with them. I understand that; it happens in a lot of families. But the disciplining of the children then falls to me.

> I tend to be firmer. The kids know that so they tend to ignore him.

> I do the disciplining. We have rules and he breaks them.

They've been more with me. He is so busy and involved with things.

Those husbands who agreed that their wives were indeed the main control agents realized that their wives spent more time with the children than they did. "She's at home; she has to do it."

But there is also the pattern whereby some of the professional wives complain that their husbands tend to overreact to children's failure to abide by the rules (the same situation appears among working-class couples). "Sometimes he is too military oriented. He is too strict, and I don't go for that." The men were also aware of this: "She says I use a sharp tone of voice when I get after the kids." The mothers are not unconcerned with discipline; they just do not want their husbands to be too rigid or too harsh with the children.

Here we need to restate a theme that surfaced in the preceding chapter. The data gained from participant observation emphasize that the nature of discipline shifts considerably as children grow older. The reactions of parents toward their children when they are young are quite different from their reactions to teenagers. A number of the couples in the professional class were acutely sensitive to the possibility of their teenage children reacting negatively to them if they were too strict and unyielding. They realized that the rules within modern urban centers are shifting rapidly and that they had to adapt to these changes. It seems to be somewhat easier for mothers than for fathers to make this adjustment.

The shifts seem most apparent with respect to daughters. The double standard of discipline for sons and for daughters in the traditional Mexican American culture has disappeared to a considerable extent. Teenage sons still have greater freedom than daughters. Nevertheless, parents have relaxed many of the formerly rigid controls on daughters. Also, daughters seem to wield considerable influence over their parents as they become adolescents. Mothers in particular are attuned to the fact that their daughters are an important emotional support for them. And the daughters realize as they become older that they can negotiate in various ways with their parents to attain certain freedoms that were unknown within the Mexican American community some decades ago. The children realize that their parents' identity depends to a degree upon their children's actions, and this realization gives them some control over parents. Professional couples are even more sensitive about their children's standing in the community than are working-class couples.

## Conclusions

My in-depth interviews and participant observation among professional women suggest a significant linkage between role making by women and the decision-making process. Professional women have come to participate more fully in a number of decision-making patterns because they have been constructing new roles for themselves within the family and the community setting. This has led most of the women to react to their husbands in a manner that is not typical of decision-making patterns in the traditional Mexican American culture, and the husbands have made some adjustments to this. In interpreting role making by professional women, it is essential to consider the constraints on role making that arise from gender and ethnicity.

It is apparent that role making by women in the professional class differs sharply from that by women in the working class. Even the most traditional women in the professional group have attained a personal and social identity that working-class women are still groping for. While one might observe some similarities in the kinds of personal struggles that these women experience within the community, the fact remains that the professional women have achieved a college education and have acquired knowledge of, and skills within, the public sphere that are still beyond the reach of working-class women.

The role making by professional Mexican American women is leading to new types of relationships with their husbands, and this is reflected in various decision-making patterns. In the area of house repairs, for instance, traditional role expectations still persist. But in other spheres, such as the purchase of furniture and the disciplining of children, professional women not only have greater influence and power than working-class wives but also differ markedly from their mothers and grandmothers. When the professional couples compared themselves to their parents or grandparents, their perception of the change that has occurred is very real.

Some further observations are in order. Even though changes have occurred in the power relationships between men and women, the relationship is still not an egalitarian one. Overall, husbands exert more power and influence than wives. Nevertheless, the decision-making process is much more complex than most scholars of decision making have been willing to entertain. The interdependence of husbands and wives and their complex negotiations in the area of, for example, furniture buying and the rearing of children suggest that the nature of decision making requires considerable reevaluation. The observations that children socialize their parents and that parents (especially mothers) depend on the approval of their children for their identity and definition of self-worth are given insufficient attention by students of the family. This situation is related to the fact that decision making between spouses may undergo revision as they go through their life course. The couples are responding both to internal dynamics within the family and to shifts in the broader society. I elaborate on these and other theoretical problems in the concluding chapter.

# Chapter 7  CONCLUSIONS AND IMPLICATIONS

This chapter briefly summarizes the principal findings of the present study, then integrates the main theoretical strands that have been utilized in the analysis and indicates why a considerably revised form of symbolic interaction theory can further the study not only of the Mexican American family but of family life in general. The suggested reformulation of this theoretical orientation should also prove advantageous in interpreting social activities in realms other than the family.

When discussing theoretical issues, it becomes necessary to be more explicit regarding the role of ethnicity in shaping the family life of Mexican Americans or Chicanos. This matter, as we see, links back, at least in part, to the symbolic interactionist framework.

As I have examined specific problem areas relating to the Mexican American family, I have introduced key concepts that are relevant for the analysis of the data in question. A detailed theoretical analysis early on would have diverted attention from my main goal, namely, to present empirical data that will provide readers with a basic understanding of contemporary Mexican American family life. Whenever feasible, I have used the voice of the respondents who have been part of this investigation. I began this research with the premise that we must understand how members of the working class and the business/professional class are defining and redefining tradition and change in extended and conjugal family arrangements.

Another goal of this research effort has been to make a theoretical contribution to the study of family life. I have suggested how symbolic interactionism, as it has typically been employed, must be modified if we are adequately to interpret changing familial arrangements within a significant sector of the Mexican American ethnic group.

## Empirical Findings

By way of a reminder, I have focused on the socially and economically more privileged sector of the Mexican American community. The data I have collected are based on research in Austin and Corpus Christi, Texas (and, to an extent, the Kingsville region as well). We must be cautious in assuming that the patterns delineated hold for all Mexican Americans in the

United States. For example, some of the patterns that have emerged from my field data are not likely to hold for the truly economically disadvantaged; nevertheless, my interaction with persons in the Kingsville region indicates that many of the general, although not necessarily the specific, changes in extended and conjugal family patterns are occurring within this group as well. I have focused primarily on the age group 25-50; if I had included older couples in the study, other patterns would have come to the fore. Then, too, my emphasis has been on married couples—not widowed, divorced, or single persons. I have not examined Mexican Americans who have intermarried with Anglos. Even with these qualifications, this work seems to be the most wide-ranging yet available on changes in the extended and conjugal family forms among Mexican Americans in contemporary urban centers.

To restate briefly some of my main findings:

1. I have provided a survey of traditional life-cycle rituals. Ceremonies relating to birth, marriage, and death help us place the family within the broader community setting, and they lead us to consider some of the basic religious beliefs and values that have been an integral part of Mexican American culture. These traditional rituals have, in the words of Eliade (1957), sustained, and been sustained by, the idea of sacred time—they have, in the perception of persons performing these activities, an eternal quality.

Social scientists often speak of the family as a central feature of Mexican American culture, but apparently no one has systematized the data regarding traditional family patterns. I do so by analyzing the rites of passage surrounding birth, marriage, and death. These highlight the functions of the extended family and provide us with an understanding of the important gender-role patterns. This knowledge is useful in its own right. It is also of theoretical and practical importance for interpreting the changes that have transpired within the extended and conjugal family systems. The data regarding traditional life-cycle rituals become the standard by which we are able to evaluate just what kinds of modifications in family life have occurred, especially with respect to extended kinship relations and gender roles. We must recognize that in the past there was a close connection among life-cycle rituals, religion, and familial integration, a linkage that has been dissolving in recent decades.

2. The extended family—*la familia*—has been given special consideration by most social scientists who write about Mexican American culture. A number of them still discuss Mexican Americans as if they continue to maintain extended family arrangements. My field observations indicate that the extended family has been disappearing, and among economically advantaged Mexican Americans in urban centers, the extended family is not central to the routines of everyday life.

If we look at specific rituals, we find that the compadrazgo ceremony, which has been associated with birth and which once led to the creation of a meaningful "fictive kinship system," has been transformed as a result of urbanization, industrialization, and bureaucratization (both in the corporate and the governmental spheres). Yet persons still cling, through a collective memory of traditional arrangements, to certain aspects of this ritual; for example, they wish to have their children baptized. But nowadays there is a strong tendency for relatives—especially brothers or sisters of the child's parents—to serve as the madrinas and padrinos. If friends act as sponsors, few expectations are attached to these roles.

As for the marriage ceremony, it no longer brings the extended family together. Thus the funeral ceremony remains as the last bastion for sustaining extended kinship arrangements. The Mexican Americans I studied observed that nowadays they meet many uncles, aunts, and cousins only at funerals. As a result, the mutual aid once associated with the extended kinship system is no longer characteristic of everyday life.

Today, Mexican Americans are caught up in the web of bureaucratic urban life. There is not only considerable mobility among family members but also the routines demanded by work, school, and the like do not permit persons to take off lengthy periods of time to attend funerals and engage in mourning activities. Mourning patterns represent a dramatic break with the past. Widows, for example, are no longer expected to wear black or to remain isolated from broader community activities.

Although the similarities between the working class and the professional class are considerable, the latter seems to attach less religious meaning to life-cycle rituals than do the former. This indirectly affects the kinship arrangements, if for no other reason than that the working class has a stronger symbolic link with tradition.

In addition, the data suggest a considerable generational gap—in the collective memory of traditional ceremonies—between persons in their late 30s and 40s and those in their 20s and early 30s. This holds both for the working and the professional classes. Within a short span of time, a loss of memory of traditional ceremonial activities has occurred, and this is reflected in the manner in which these ceremonies are conducted and the meanings that family members attach to them.

3. If one compares the current patterns regarding power relationships between husbands and wives with those in traditional Mexican American culture, major shifts can be discerned (although we should be mindful of the diversity that has been documented in earlier chapters).

My research points to the persistence of male dominance within Mexican American families, but this pattern is less prominent than in the past. The stereotypical role of the husband and father as having total control was exaggerated in earlier research (Madsen 1964; Rubel 1966). Yet the patriarchy that existed some decades ago has been undermined to some extent in the working and professional classes in urban centers. At the same time, an egalitarian relationship between husband and wife, which some researchers have claimed exists, is not supported by the data I have collected. Husbands continue to wield greater power than their wives.

My thesis is that we cannot understand what has transpired in the relationship between husbands and wives unless we take account of role making, especially by women. Although Mexican Americans are struggling to adapt to broader social forces, they are also active agents in remaking roles for themselves. My fieldwork materials indicate that we cannot understand decision-making patterns among couples unless we first examine the new roles that have been created—a fact implicit, but not made theoretically explicit, in current research studies on the family. Moreover, we cannot understand decision-making patterns unless we take account of the various types of resistance that Mexican Americans, especially women, experience as they strive to restructure traditional role expectations.

That important differences in the power relationship between husbands and wives can be found between working-class and professional couples is not an unexpected finding. But these patterns have not been documented in the literature on Mexican Americans. Working-class women are striving to establish a personal and social identity apart from that of their husbands; these women are breaking from the traditional culture wherein a woman's identity stemmed from being solely a wife and a mother. Women in the professional class take their newfound sense of personal and social identity for granted. Furthermore, these women display a considerable variety of role-making activities; the economic opportunity structures outside the home are greater for them than for their working-class counterparts. Overall, professional women exert more influence and power in specific decision-making areas than do working-class women.

4. A fourth body of findings, which are related to points 2 and 3, concerns role making by married women who are twice a minority. As in other sectors of U.S. society, women are taking the lead in remaking their conjugal roles. When we examine the situation of Mexican American women as twice a minority, however, we must recognize that they encounter restrictions not only as a result of their gender (a problem they share with women in the majority sector) but also as a result of their ethnicity. My field observations suggest that working-class women are more likely to be discriminated against in the community as a result of their ethnicity than as a result of their gender, whereas professional women experience this somewhat more in terms of their gender than in terms of their ethnicity. But often these women are unable to sort out the interactive effects of these constraints on their role making.

As a result of their position in the broader community and organizational setting, Mexican American women must rely more heavily on the family for emotional support than their Anglo counterparts. In addition, these women must learn to live with contradictory role expectations unknown to women in the majority sector (a point to which we return below). While Mexican American husbands are experiencing tensions in the process of remaking their roles, these are not as marked for them as for their wives.

## Rethinking Theoretical Issues in the Study of the Family

I have focused on changing role patterns in the extended and conjugal families of Mexican Americans. But to understand change, one must also understand tradition. In order to interpret the revisions that have occurred in the Mexican American family I have found it essential to modify and extend the symbolic interactionist perspective in a variety of ways. These theoretical reformulations have resulted from an effort to interpret and explain more adequately what the respondents were saying and doing. It is now essential partially to weave together the key concepts that I have introduced into my analysis to interpret the data not only on traditional life-cycle rituals but also on the changes that have occurred in the extended and conjugal families during the past several decades.

### Revisions in Symbolic Interaction Theory

Symbolic interaction in its essential core recognizes that human beings are social in nature. The definition of one's "self" and one's "mind" emerges out of interaction with others, and the meaning that husbands and wives attach to objects and other persons is likewise a result of ongoing interaction with these. From the standpoint of symbolic interactionism, there are no truly "isolated" human beings; how persons define themselves and others is a product of ongoing interaction with others. The definition of independent individuals that is so romanticized in U.S. culture, and often accepted as a reality by many social scientists, does not conform to empirical reality.

Symbolic interactionism stands in contrast to social exchange theories. While some versions of exchange theories incorporate symbolic interaction concepts (see, for example, Moschetti 1979), this is the exception rather than the rule. Most modern exchange theory is based on operant learning theory models (see, for example, Emerson 1972; Cook and Emerson 1978; Molm 1987) or classical economic models[1] (see, for example, Blau 1964) and consequently incorporates the assumptions of these models. As a result, exchange theory, because the theory is highly abstract, does not consider specific types of resources (for an exception, see Foa and Foa 1974). Thus, most exchange theory cannot deal with intricacies of many types of social behavior, especially intimate relationships. For example, the market of classical economic models does not seem to capture properties of loyalty, trust, and equity considerations (see Cook and Emerson 1978 for discussion).

Exchange theory assumes that persons inevitably strive to act in accordance with "self-interest." Although social exchange or preferably, the idea of reciprocity (Gouldner 1960), exists within family settings, what is self-interest is subject to a greater variety of interpretations than most exchange theorists are willing to recognize. Also, human agents depend on others for support and sustenance in order to exist. The interdependency relationships that arise in, for example, family situations cannot be ignored. Young children in particular depend on the altruism of their parents if they are to survive.

Symbolic interactionism has also been contrasted with structural functionalism. In its extreme form, the actor has disappeared from the analyses of certain adherents to this framework. While Talcott Parsons (1937) and Merton (1968) have taken the human actor into account, this actor is not the active, creative agent that one finds stressed in symbolic interactionism — the creative agent who, for instance, strives to remake and redefine existing roles. Yet there are aspects of the structural functional tradition, going back to Emile Durkheim (1915), on which we must draw, for Durkheim's analysis of tradition and rituals cannot be overlooked by symbolic interactionists (Collins 1988).

One major modification in the use of symbolic interactionism calls for placing human beings within some historical context. Mead (1938) recognized the role of the past, and, more recently, some symbolic interactionists have been rediscovering the importance of social time. But Blumer (1969) in his most influential essays ignored this facet of human life. But we cannot understand social change within the family (or other social spheres) from a symbolic interactionist perspective without an explicit recognition of the historical process, including understanding the role of tradition in its various forms. If we are to write about the remaking of roles, and the restructuring of the role sets that exist within the extended and the conjugal families, we must be aware of the nature of the roles that are being redefined (Williams 1988).

It is difficult to examine the historical process of family life without considering how broader religious beliefs and values, such as those relating to religion, have shaped familial arrangements. This becomes salient for studying such an ethnic group as Mexican Americans. How these beliefs and values are interpreted as persons engage in role making within a variety of family settings must be one focus of attention.

In taking account of the historical process, and the notion of social time, we must also consider the broader structural arrangements that affect family life, and which family members play a role in reshaping. McCall and Simmons (1982) have taken a major step in bringing these issues into the symbolic interactionist framework, but we must do more with what they have initiated. Just how the members of the Mexican American extended and conjugal families are remaking — and failing to remake (as a result of resistance by others) — their roles within the context of community, organizational, and societal arrangements must be addressed. Patterns within the family cannot be examined if we treat the family as isolated from the shifting social arrangements within the broader community, society, or even global setting.

Bureaucratic structures (e.g., the school system, the governmental apparatus, or corporate entities) deeply affect the nature of family life. My research indicates that the routinization and standardization imposed by these organizations have affected such rituals as funerals, and these organizational structures often restrict the role-making activities of both men and women. This in turn affects relationships within the family. Although some scholars conceive of the family as an emotional haven (Lasch 1977), organizational structures intrude into family activities, and symbolic interactionists must come to terms with the various ways in which persons, including family members, interpret or partially reshape the impact of those organizations on their everyday life.[2]

One of the most significant theoretical modifications that must be made in the symbolic interaction framework, as it has been applied during the past four or five decades, is to stress the place of the "social mind," not just the "social self" or social or personal identity. Particularly as a result of Blumer's influence, symbolic interactionists have given primary attention to the notion of the social self. Even his critics within symbolic interactionism (e.g., Stryker 1980) have emphasized the self. However, Mead discussed the social mind in his book *Mind, Self and Society* (1934). Today, the role of the mind is being given increased attention in areas such as cognitive psychology (Sanford 1987). And the idea of the social mind is surely being reintroduced into some versions of symbolic interactionism (Collins 1989; Vaughan and Sjoberg 1984).

We must recognize that human beings think, and they reflect about how they think. Although certain biological capacities are essential for the existence of the mind, the thinking process is nonetheless socially created in the process of interaction, and no less so than is the social self. The social mind engages in complex social calculations, and it is also the basis of social memory (without which the importance of tradition in social relationships cannot be grasped). Through a variety of social calculations, which often are interwoven with such emotions as empathy, we are able to take the roles of others. We imagine, relying on verbal and other cues, how others perceive us and then draw on our social memory of past experiences; reasoning from these, typically through analogy, we respond to others accordingly. It is social memory of past interactions that permits us to interact with persons whom we have not previously encountered.

Within this context, we can go back to our data and take note of the generational differences that have emerged among Mexican Americans in the communities that I studied. Mexican Americans in their late 30s and 40s remember many more of the traditional life-cycle forms than do younger ones, and this memory has a bearing on the nature of their family experiences. Without the concept of the social mind, we would find it impossible to utilize the concept of memory, including the collective memory of social traditions, in interpreting the actions of men and women in the Mexican American family. In addition, the loss of collective memory regarding rituals is reshaping the way young couples interact with extended family members.

Knowledge about Mexican Americans' reflective processes is necessary if we are to understand the negotiation process that goes on within families. Yet we must be careful not to overemphasize the role of reflectivity, for habit — and taken-for-granted assumptions about ordinary life — shapes the way in which spouses respond to each other. At times, when asked about decision making, couples simply noted that they "came to an agreement" about, for example, the purchase of an item of furniture. But how they came to that agreement is not easy for them to reconstruct, for after years of living together, they have come to depend on subtle cues and personal habits and tastes that are taken as givens and are difficult for them to conceptualize. In this situation, observation by a third party over time may be necessary for understanding what has transpired. Negotiation between spouses is not equivalent to negotiation between union leaders and corporate executives. One reason that limited progress has been made in understanding decision making between couples is because we have not taken into account reflective thought (and the social calculations associated with it) on the one hand and habitual action on the other.

Finally, symbolic interactionists, as suggested above, must recognize the existence of contradictory role expectations in everyday life (Billig et al. 1988). The contradictions faced by Mexican Americans exist within the familial setting and especially within the community and broader society. Lal (1986), citing Blumer and Duster, suggests that this notion has crept into symbolic interactionism, for Blumer and Duster discuss tensions resulting from emulation of the majority by the minority as opposed to the latter's maintenance of ethnic identity.

But we must further examine contradictory role expectations if we are to understand the dynamics of Mexican American family life. Mexican

American married women, in particular, are faced with contradictory expectations. They must cope with the traditional expectations associated with being a good wife and mother and with the emerging expectations associated with their work world outside the home. The reactions to their gender and ethnicity generate still other contradictions. Although many persons, especially in the majority sector, assert that equality of opportunity exists in practice, Mexican American women or Chicanas are often negated for their gender, often for their ethnicity, at times for both. Thus they must learn to live with cognitive dissonance (cf. Aronson 1988). They cannot escape the contradictions and must learn to manage them if they are to sustain their social identity and social stability; they cannot cope with them simply through compartmentalization of various activities (Goode 1973). Members of ethnic minorities learn to live with a degree of turmoil and social pain that members of the majority never experience. The pain of being rejected as a human being is severe.

In sum, symbolic interactionism, if it is to advance our knowledge of the family, must recognize that interaction occurs within a historical framework (which leads us to take account of social time) as well as the broader community and organizational setting. Social interaction among family members does not occur in isolation from this wider context. Moreover, symbolic interactionists must focus not only on the social self but also on the social mind with its capacity for reflective thought (and social calculations) as well as social or collective memory. Certainly we must recognize that Mexican American family members not only are adapting to change but also are seeking to remake their roles in the face of upheavals within the contemporary social order. In turn, the idea of role making leads us back to a consideration of change over time and to organizational constraints on role making. Finally, to understand the roles of Mexican American men and, especially, women, we must come to terms with the ambiguities and contradictory expectations that they experience in everyday life.

### Ethnicity

Throughout, we have emphasized that a considerably modified version of symbolic interactionism can add greatly to an understanding of the nature of family life within ethnic groups. Implicit in my analysis are certain views regarding ethnicity that need to be stated more explicitly; this links back into the modified symbolic interactionist framework I have developed.

We must understand that the dominant model for interpreting ethnic groups in the United States is still the assimilationist model, especially that advanced by Gordon (1964). His framework is dominant in the field of race and ethnic studies, including the work of persons studying family life in ethnic groups. Many of these scholars assume that current changes in ethnic families result from the fact that the members of these ethnic groups are attempting to become like Anglos.

But there are sound empirical and theoretical reasons for questioning the validity of the assimilationist model. In my own research I encountered only one couple who explicitly wanted to become assimilated. There are other Mexican Americans who view assimilation in a positive light. Rodriguez (1982), in his *Hunger of Memory*, champions this point of view. Nevertheless, he, along with many social scientists, ignores certain basic social facts. How can we neglect to treat the definition of the situation by most Mexican Americans — that is, that they do not accept the assimilationist model? Is the majority's perspective the only one that social scientists are willing to adopt?

Another major question arises with respect to the assimilationist perspective: How is it possible for Mexican Americans to be assimilated into the Anglo social and cultural order when they are being discriminated against in a variety of ways? The majority wants minority members to become like them, but at the same time they subject these persons to various forms of exclusion. It is true that the degree of exclusion nowadays is not as severe as it was some decades ago; however, various forms of segregation continue to exist. Thus San Miguel (1987:216) writes that "in the 1980s Mexican Americans continued to be placed in segregated and inferior schools, in vocational programs, and in remedial programs." Given the fact that the United States has become a credential-oriented society, exclusion through education deeply affects the lives of Mexican Americans.

As a result of the continuing negation of Mexican Americans by the majority sector, Mexican Americans' identification with their culture serves as a buffer against the onslaught to self. To the extent that one gains an identity from one's particular culture, one is able to carve out a somewhat more meaningful existence.

The nature of ethnic identity has consequences for the nature of the self and for role making. I have not addressed this matter directly in the preceding chapters, in part because the issues lie somewhat beyond the boundaries of the problem as I originally defined it. But at this point I introduce certain issues that are an extension of the data I have presented on Mexican American family life, especially in the conjugal unit.

In recent years, a group of social scientists (e.g., Zurcher 1977, 1986a; Turner 1976) have argued that persons in the United States are increasingly developing their sense of self not from any institutional identification but from one based on impulse. For a number of years, I grappled with the fact that the patterns that Zurcher and Turner are describing do not really help me to interpret how Mexican Americans define themselves. Individualism has emerged among Mexican Americans, but it is not the individualism documented by Turner and Zurcher. My field data do not lend support to the views advanced by these sociologists. At the least, their theoretical orientations must be reformulated if they are to apply to the groups I have studied. One reason appears to be that most Mexican Americans still have a strong sense of ethnic identity, which in turn is associated with a relatively strong sense of community. Consequently, they do not adopt a definition of the social self and the social mind that stresses "impulse" or "narcissism," with self-gratification as an end in itself. My research leads me to conclude that certain role-making patterns among Mexican American working-class and professional class couples do not conform to those in the privileged sectors of Anglo society, in part because of the majority sector's exclusion of ethnic minorities.

These issues are related to current debates about the family, especially regarding women's roles, in U.S. society. Cancian (1987), for example, criticizes a range of scholars (e.g., Bellah et al. 1985; Lasch 1978) whom she claims have failed to recognize the advantages for women of "self-development" or the "human potential movement." Cancian casts the empirical trends described by Turner and Zurcher in a positive light; she views these as providing women with greater freedom and social opportunities. For her, scholars who stress the need for a sense of community have a more restricted view of the potential of women within the society as a whole.

Much of the debate that has been generated by the patterns regarding the nature of the self as defined by Zurcher and Turner—for example, Bellah et al. on the one side and Cancian on the other—centers on the future of the family and of women in the privileged majority sector. Unfortunately, Bellah's concern with community does not explicitly embrace ethnic minorities. And Cancian's concern with the human potential movement does not consider how this pattern may lead advantaged persons to push minorities aside in order to further their own position. In general, these writers have adopted the premises of the assimilationist model, for they assume, often implicitly, that minorities can or should be like the majority. They do not take the role of disadvantaged minorities and do not attempt to understand the social world from the perspective of those who are being excluded from the advantages of the privileged sector.

This discussion leads me to address other problems that directly and indirectly are a by-product of the assimilationist world view. I have given considerable attention in this book to Mexican American women as twice a minority. How this issue is partially linked into the assimilationist framework requires elaboration.

Looking closely at contemporary women's studies, and particularly the feminist perspective, we see that much of the research and analysis has rested on the assumption of "sisterhood." The idea, which emerged from the women's movement in the 1960s, is that women share certain basic commonalities that transcend class and ethnic boundaries. While I recognize that women may share certain concerns and interests, the limitations of the central premise of sisterhood are becoming increasingly apparent. For example, Fox-Genovese (1988), a prominent historian, has challenged this orientation in her research on southern plantation women in the United States. She demonstrates that white women were the oppressors, black women the oppressed. White women profited from having black women as slaves.

Fox-Genovese has brought into sharp focus an important issue that many scholars, including sociologists, have suppressed.[3] Only a few studies in sociology have examined the fact that the differences between privileged Anglo women and women of color may be greater than the similarities. It is generally accepted that the women's movement was a product of the activities of privileged Anglo women, and women in the social sciences have been part of this. But in the process, compelling problems encountered by disadvantaged women in general, and women of color in particular, have been overlooked. Lengermann and Niebrugge-Brantley (1988:311), in their recent survey of feminist theory, lend support to issues raised by Fox-Genovese. After reviewing the major conceptual themes in feminist theory, they conclude:

> There is a growing concern within feminist theory over the exploitation of women of one class, race, ethnic group, or global position by women of another. In other words, a new question is emerging for feminist theorists: *"And what about differences among women?"* (Italics in Original.)

This general issue is relevant not just for feminist theory but also for sociological theory and for the analysis of the family. Also, the reason for analyzing this controversy within this context is that the emphasis on "sisterhood" is a particular variant of the assimilationist model that has been so prevalent among social scientists in the United States. Generalizations about family life and women's gender roles in the United States have often been based on research on the white middle class, and it is then assumed that minority women are like those in the privileged group.

In order to correct social scientists' overidentification with the assimilationist model, we must consider seriously a central aspect of symbolic interactionist theory: taking the role of the other. If this perspective is applied properly, researchers must grapple with the difficult task of taking the roles of persons who are different from themselves, including minorities that many members of the majority sector tacitly reject. Unfortunately, most sociologists, including symbolic interactionists, have not wrestled with the theoretical and methodological difficulties associated with taking the roles of "outsiders" (Williams 1989b). It is often taken for granted that the social researcher is readily able to do so. But how many researchers are comfortable with persons who are truly different from themselves?

### An Alternative to the Assimilationist Model

In this book I have proceeded on the principle — supported by my field research, other social science research on minorities, as well as theoretical analysis — that the assimilationist model is inadequate for interpreting social change, particularly role making within the extended and conjugal family arrangements among Mexican Americans. Mexican Americans have become acculturated into the U.S. social order, and some are being assimilated. But most Mexican Americans are not assimilated. The assimilationist world view looks at the social order from the top down and does not take account of the social realities as seen from the minority perspective.

At this point, I advance a theoretical alternative to the assimilationist model, one that has been implicit throughout this book. The thesis is that both Mexican Americans and Anglo families are responding to major changes on the societal and global levels. I perceive these social forces as involving industrialization (including scientific developments) urbanization, and the bureaucratization of modern life (Goode 1970; Popenoe 1988). Mexican Americans live in a capitalist economic order; however, capitalism is anchored within the context of large-scale organizations (e.g., Galbraith 1971). As I have noted, these organizations — with their hierarchy of authority, division of labor, and emphasis on standardization and efficiency — have restructured people's family life in dramatic ways and will likely continue to do so. We can expect that the intervention by the state and the corporate sector will continue to increase and thus have an even greater impact on the family in the future. Moreover, we recognize that scientific and technological change will continue to accelerate, and both Mexican Americans and Anglo families will be affected by unforeseen developments. For example, new birth control and abortion techniques, as well as reproductive technologies, are having, or will likely have, important ramifications for family life in some sectors of U.S. society. Also, modern technology and large-scale organizations are fostering a global economic order that, too, will impact on the family.

Along with these ongoing structural changes have been revisions in the cultural and, notably, the belief system. These cultural changes are interwoven in complex ways with fundamental structural changes on the societal and global scenes. Traditional religious beliefs have been undermined to some degree by the broad-scale educational revolution that has been associated with the rise of science and technology. With respect to Mexican Americans, more specifically, one can hypothesize that changes initiated by Pope John in the 1960s have at least had an indirect influence on the family life of this minority group. Church doctrine and rituals have been modified to some degree.

The structural and cultural changes are also reflected in social-psychological patterns in the United States.[4] I have referred to the redefinition of the self from one based on institutional identification to one based on impulse.

The structural, cultural, and social-psychological changes and their impact on the family have been associated with intensive political debate about the nature and future of family life in the United States. The intensity of the debate is particularly pronounced in the area of abortion but is reflected in many other facets of family life as well (Farber 1987).

Some of the dramatic shifts in the nature of social life in the United States have been captured by Studs Terkel (1988) in his book *The Great Divide*. He perceives a considerable generation gap within U.S. society as a result of the social upheavals of the past several decades. These changes are reflected to a degree in the Mexican American community, for in various sections of this book I have discussed the generational differences between Mexican Americans in their 20s and early 30s and those in their 40s with respect to the collective memory of the traditional cultural heritage. In this realm, persons in their 40s have more in common with older Mexican Americans than with younger persons.[5] Mexican Americans have not been insulated from the shifts that have occurred on the societal and global levels.

Nevertheless, Mexican Americans and Anglos are responding to these structural and cultural changes in different ways. They are responding differently because of their divergent positions in the societal order. For example, the privileged Anglos and Mexican Americans in general are very likely to be at odds with each other regarding various political debates about family issues. In addition, we must recognize that familial patterns in different classes of Anglos and Mexican Americans are not the same. I have constantly emphasized that Mexican Americans are not a homogeneous social entity.

More specifically, I have stressed that role making by Mexican American women is constrained by the fact that, unlike Anglo women, they are twice a minority. Moreover, Mexican American working-class women differ in their role-making patterns from professional women.

That Mexican Americans are not simply emulating Anglos is underlined by the data on funerals. There is a considerable body of empirical findings indicating that funeral patterns within the Anglo society are taking on new social forms.[6] Funeral ceremonies among Mexican Americans are also undergoing change. But the major issue then becomes: How can Mexican Americans be emulating patterns that are still emerging and ill defined within the Anglo society (Williams 1987)? A far more adequate sociological explanation of this kind of social situation involves an explicit recognition that although Anglos and Mexican Americans are responding to common social forces, they are doing so in different ways.[7] By reconceptualizing the problem in this manner, we are able to avoid some of the serious pitfalls that inhere in the assimilationist model, and we can do justice to explaining the nature of family forms in both the Anglo and the Mexican American sectors of U.S. society.

## Concluding Remarks

My primary objective has been to add to our empirical knowledge about the Mexican American family in particular, and Mexican American everyday life more generally. I have done so through a greatly modified and revised symbolic interactionist perspective.

I have described in some detail the revisions that have been occurring in the extended and conjugal family systems. These have been dramatic in recent decades. Nevertheless, we can expect even greater modifications to occur in the future, and the process of documenting the ongoing patterns is never complete. Yet I have striven to provide future researchers with data on contemporary urban family life on which they can build in future investigations of this second largest minority group in the United States. It is a group about which we have relatively little social scientific knowledge.

The advancement of knowledge about Mexican Americans has not only theoretical but also practical implications. The kind of data that has been reported in this work has relevance for broad policy issues. We cannot hope, for example, to come to terms with the high dropout rate of Mexican Americans from the school system until we gain basic understanding of the interrelationships among the family, the community, and the schools. In fact, knowledge about the family is fundamental to the formulation of a wide variety of programs that will advance the quality of life among disadvantaged ethnic groups, including Mexican Americans.

We must also recognize that ethnic diversity within the United States seems to be increasing rather than decreasing. The number of Hispanics, including Mexican Americans, will grow dramatically in the next few decades. This situation calls for understanding the multicultural nature of U.S. society so that diverse groups will come to interact with one another in a more humane and just manner.

## Notes

1. The dominance of the economic perspective can be seen in, for example, Bean and Swicegood (1985). Some sociologists, such as Collins (1988:13-15), seem to attempt to integrate exchange theory with "situational negotiation and reality construction," but I am not persuaded that this theoretical linkage is supported by their analysis. For other versions of the use of exchange theory on the study of family life, see Blood and Wolfe (1960) and Scanzoni and Szinovacz (1980).

2. My emphasis upon bureaucratic structures must not be confused with the structural symbolic interactionism of Stryker (1980). Stryker has criticized Blumer for his emphasis on the fluidity and emergence of human interaction. But his discussion of structure does not encompass the larger bureaucratic organizations that affect the nature of people's personality. I have argued elsewhere that there is a bureaucratic personality (Williams et al. 1983), and we need to know how this personality pattern influences the manner in which persons relate to one another in family settings. My observations suggest that personality patterns shaped in the public sphere influence how family members, especially husbands and wives, react to one another in the private sphere.

3. One can cite a large body of literature on women that overlooks minority women. A recent example is Hess and Ferree's (1987) edited book, *Analyzing Gender: A Handbook of Social Science Research*. This work seeks to present a comprehensive summary of research on the study of women, but we find that Hispanic women, especially Mexican Americans, are mentioned only in passing. To paraphrase Escobedo (1980), Mexican American women, who are members of the second largest minority group in the United States, are often perceived by social scientists as a "nonexistent minority."

Atkinson (1987:20) lends support to my thesis, for she observes that research on gender roles within the family has been based on data from the white middle class.

4. Implicit throughout my theoretical analysis is a set of assumptions regarding the relationship of the micro to the macro social order. The debate about this issue has been an intensive one in social theory during the 1980s (see, e.g., Alexander et al. 1987). I cannot examine the complexities of this problem herein. My own views come close to that set forth by Vaughan and Sjoberg (1984).

5. For data that lend support to my observations, see Schultz et al. 1988.

6. For a discussion of modifications in funeral ceremonies within the broader U.S. society, see, e.g., Payne 1984.

7. Our critique of the assimilationist model especially with respect to Mexican Americans can be approached from still another perspective, the complexities of which lie beyond the scope of this study.

It is significant that in the southwestern United States, particularly in Texas, certain features of the Anglo cultural tradition had their origins in the culture of Mexico; these features in turn were perpetuated by Mexican Americans who became citizens of the United States after the Treaty of Guadalupe Hidalgo in 1848. For example, many aspects of the cowboy culture—romanticized in Anglo film, literature, and song—were borrowed from Mexico mainly via the Mexican American population (cf. Jackson 1986). Also, certain Anglo legal patterns, including some relating to the family, were adopted from the Mexican tradition on the frontier. What I am suggesting is that these cultural patterns would not have become so deeply embedded within the dominant or mainstream culture had it not been for the existence of a sizable population of Mexican Americans in the United States after the 1848 treaty with Mexico.

Those who advocate an assimilationist model are, without realizing it, arguing that Mexican Americans are emulating certain cultural traditions that may be more Mexican American than Anglo in character. Given this situation, adherents of the assimilationist perspective should reexamine what they mean by assimilation into particular cultural traditions.

**A METHODOLOGICAL NOTE**

This appendix elaborates on the data set forth in the Introduction. Although it repeats certain facts regarding the research design, it presents many additional details as well.

I began this project on an informal basis in the summer of 1979 and ended it in the spring of 1987. During that period, I was in the field at times on a part-time basis, on other occasions on a full-time basis. My main research sites were Austin and Corpus Christi, Texas. I also obtained considerable data on family life in the Kingsville region, including Falfurrias. Also, I collected data on Mexican American family life when I lived with a family for part of one summer in a small town south of San Antonio.

What follows is an examination of the procedures I used in collecting the data in analyzing my findings. Inasmuch as this research is qualitative in nature, I have built on the efforts of social scientists who have worked within that framework (e.g., Lofland and Lofland 1984; Denzin 1989a; Whyte 1984).

### Data Collection

The data were collected primarily through in-depth interviews and participant observation. In addition, some use was made of "objectifying interviews."

#### In-depth interviews

I interviewed 75 couples in Austin and Corpus Christi, Texas. Austin was selected primarily for pragmatic reasons, for I resided there at the time. My choice of Corpus Christi was more deliberate. I set out to replicate my Austin research in a city in South Texas that was not on the border and that had a large Mexican American population.

My primary focus has been couples in the working class and in the business/professional group (I use the word "professional" as a synonym for business/professional). I chose to focus on the economically privileged sector of the Mexican American community, for I have assumed that the most rapid changes in the familial system have occurred within this group.

Still, some data were collected on lower-class families as a result of my observations in Kingsville.

Occupation and education were the two criteria employed to delineate social class. With respect to the professional group, I selected couples in which at least one spouse had a college degree and the other some college education. For the working class, I selected couples who had completed at least five years of elementary school and had not had a college education.

I carried out informal research in the years 1979 through 1983, especially during the summers, in the Kingsville region, and I began my formal study in Austin in the fall of 1981 and completed it in late 1983. (I did not live in Austin in the summers.) During this period I interviewed 22 couples in the working class and 21 couples in the professional class.

The members of the working class in Austin more than met the minimum educational standards I had established before undertaking the research. In fact, 31 of the 44 persons had a high school diploma. To the extent that education is an indicator of class, it is clear that this group was among the more advantaged element of the working class.

The men worked in a rather wide range of occupations. Two were mechanics, and 2 were printers. Among the other occupations represented were barber, air-conditioner installer, lab assistant, and laborer on a road repair crew.

Only 2 of the women had never worked. There were a number of secretaries and clerks, and such occupations as babysitter, seamstress, teacher's aide, and tester of burglar alarms were represented.

With respect to the professional class, in 15 couples both spouses had at least one college degree (some had advanced degrees). In all other instances, one spouse had a college degree and the other some college education (among the latter, a few were in college at the time of the interview).

Among the men in the professional class, almost half were working for a governmental agency in a variety of capacities; a few were consultants for the public sector. Other occupations represented were nurse, insurance agent, and members of the financial community.

All the professional women had at one time been employed, although 4 were not working at the time of the interview. Some were public school teachers, and several held administrative posts in the public sector. Other occupations included, for instance, nurse, librarian, editor, and speech therapist.

I also sought to interview persons who fell into the general age category 25 to 50. While some age diversity within the sample was desirable, I excluded younger and elderly couples in order to make the research manageable.

The Austin sample included persons in age groups 25-29, 30-39, and 40-50. I included 2 couples in the working class and 2 in the professional group in which the wives were in their 40s and the husbands 51 or 52 years of age. (I interviewed one couple in their mid-50s whom I have not included in the analysis.) As for family size, the working class had more children than did the professional group. In the former, all the couples had children: 4 couples had 1-2 children; 15 couples had 3-4; and 3 couples had 5-7. In the professional class, 3 had no children (2 couples were in their 20s); 11 couples had 1-2 children; 6 couples had 3-4; and one couple had 5.

I entered the working- and professional-class groups at different contact points. I then used a snowball sample, as respondents referred me to couples who would likely agree to be interviewed (Bailey 1987). By entering each class through different social contacts, I was able to interview a number of couples in each group who did not know one another. Although my research is not based on a probability sample, I am, because of my participant observation, confident that I interviewed a rather diverse group of persons within each class.

One special issue regarding the sample in Austin should be mentioned. I included one working-class couple in which the wife had come to the United States from Mexico in her teens and was married to a Mexican American. In two other instances, one of the spouses had come to the United States as an infant and the other before the age of 2. Another person had entered the country at the age of 3. These last three respondents were unaware of any extended family in Mexico; thus the only country they have known has been the United States. All 4 respondents were naturalized citizens and defined themselves as Mexican Americans. (All the persons in the Corpus Christi sample were born here.) Most of the persons I interviewed were typically second- to fourth-generation Mexican Americans.

Having discussed the sample in Austin, I turn to an analysis of the interviewing process. I used a rather lengthy interview guide as the basis for asking questions of both husbands and wives. With rare exceptions, each spouse was interviewed separately. Many qualitative researchers have been criticized for the failure to standardize their data-collection procedures; the interview guide was an effort to overcome this objection. While I did ask certain questions of all respondents, I was intent on using the interview guide as the basis for probing in depth regarding changes in the extended and conjugal family patterns. I thus followed up many questions with additional questions or comments (Snow et al. 1982). The follow-up questions were essential for gathering information about many kinds of familial patterns. Typically, the interviews lasted for three to four hours, and in a number of cases they were completed only after several visits. This pattern of interviewing over time proved to be informative, for it facilitated the collection of several kinds of data. Asking persons about historical changes in life-cycle rituals is quite different from querying them about ongoing role-making and decision-making activities. The first set of questions involved reliance on the respondents' "social memory." Questions about changing life-cycle rituals, for instance, often triggered memories of past events that the respondents had not reflected upon for years. Some persons thus filled in gaps as I interviewed them over time; in some instances, people called me to provide me with additional data because the questions I asked had led them to reflect upon past events. The collection of data about a person's past experiences and knowledge poses special difficulties for social researchers (Rubin 1986). But some of these hurdles can be overcome if one realizes that the interviewer should collect information over time and use the interview as a means of assisting respondents in recalling data from the past.

At this point, a discussion of certain supplementary data is appropriate. During the summer of 1982, I interviewed five persons in their 70s and 80s in the Corpus Christi-Kingsville area regarding traditional life-cycle rituals. Going back for revisits was essential in stimulating these persons to recall details about past activities that no longer exist. Since that summer, I have interviewed a number of other elderly persons, primarily in the Kingsville region, regarding the data that appear in Chapter 2.

The description of the essential features of my sample and of the interviewing process in Corpus Christi will be briefer than that for Austin, for the second phase of my research was specifically carried out to check on the findings in Austin. My research design in Corpus Christi was similar to that employed in Austin. One difference was that the interviews were somewhat shorter, for I had by then come to focus more specifically on particular problems with respect to the family.

I interviewed 16 working class couples and 16 professional class couples in Corpus Christi. Again, I entered each class through different social contacts. I carried out most of the in-depth interviewing in the summer of 1985, and I completed it in the summer of 1986 and during periodic visits to the city in the academic years of 1985-86 and 1986-87.

In the working class, 25 out of the 32 respondents had completed high school, and the rest had completed the eighth through the eleventh grades. Within the professional group, 30 persons had a college degree (some of them had advanced degrees), and the other 2 persons had some college education.

In the working class, the men held such jobs as fireman, salesperson, repairman, mechanic, and electrician. All the wives save one had at one time been employed, and they worked in such occupations as seamstress, maid, cashier, secretary, or clerk.

Turning to the occupations of men in the professional class, one was an attorney, several occupied positions in the medical community, and another was a supervisor in a private firm. All the women except one had worked at some time or another, although 3 were not working during the period of the interview. Among those who were employed, several were teachers, another a bookkeeper, another a nurse, and so on.

All the respondents in both classes were in the age group 25 to 50, and they fall at various points along this continuum. As for children, 2 working-class couples were childless. Of the other couples, 4 had 1-2 children; 10 had 3-4 children. In the professional class, 7 couples had 1-2 children; 7 had 3-4; one couple had 5 children; and one couple did not have a child at the time of the interview.

If we compare Austin and Corpus Christi in general terms, it appears that economic opportunities are more limited in Corpus Christi than in Austin. Certainly during the early 1980s Austin was a rapidly growing and booming urban center. Moreover, the Mexican American respondents in Corpus Christi were typically born in the city or its immediate environs. Most of those in Austin, especially in the professional class, had migrated to the city from various parts of South Texas, but many had lived in Austin for many years.

### Participant Observation

In addition to carrying out in-depth interviews, I collected data in both Austin and Corpus Christi through participant observation, and I focused on the same kinds of couples as in my in-depth interviews. All the data in the Kingsville region were collected through participant observation, especially during the summers 1979 through 1983 and during periodic visits to the Corpus Christi-Kingsville region in the period 1985 to 1987. Most of these families were members of the working class, and a number occupied a rather low economic status. Also, I lived with a working-class family in a small town south of San Antonio for about one month in the summer of 1979.

As the project evolved, my participant observation took on increased significance. It provided me with an opportunity to observe families in their natural settings. In Austin I went to parties, visited couples in their homes, and engaged in a variety of community activities. For example, I participated in an arts and crafts class that consisted of working-class women. Then, too, I interacted with a number of working-class women in both cities whom I provided with assistance in dealing with special problems they faced. I view it as sound moral practice to assist respondents whenever feasible (Wax 1952).

I have also attended baptisms, weddings, and funerals in Austin, Corpus Christi, and the Kingsville region, as well as other communities in Texas. (Also, when visiting with elderly Mexican Americans from different parts of the State, I often discussed traditional life-cycle rituals with them.) My participant observation served several distinct functions:

First, it has permitted me to observe couples whom I had formally interviewed in a variety of social settings. In Austin I observed about one-third of the working-class couples and about two-thirds of the professionals outside the formal interview situation. In Corpus Christi I participated in social activities (at least to some degree) with most of the couples I had interviewed. In both cities, what persons said corresponded with what they actually did (cf. Deutscher 1973). To be sure, as I have discussed in the body of the text, persons set forth their ideal expectations and then also provided data on what they did when faced with specific situations. Overall, they were forthright in their responses.

Second, the participant observation provided me with data on couples I did not interview. Some of the couples were observed for only a brief period of time, others quite intensively. The data regarding ongoing social interaction have been invaluable in helping me sort out certain theoretical issues, especially about role making and decision making. Moreover, as noted above, in the Kingsville region I was able to observe familial patterns among some low-income Mexican American families; these background data provided me with a clearer understanding of both the working-class group and the professional class that I studied in Austin and Corpus Christi.

Third, I interacted with Mexican Americans in settings wherein I observed married men and women in their community and organizational settings, including interaction with Anglos. This knowledge is relevant for understanding Mexican Americans as an ethnic group and for coming to terms with how their ethnicity affects familial arrangements.

## The Objectifying Interview

Another source of data was the "objectifying interview." This concept, used by Sjoberg and Nett (1968), refers to situations in which respondents become "expert observers." They are informed about the nature of the project and provide the researcher with strategic data. Such a procedure was employed to some extent by Whyte (1955) in his research for *Street Corner Society*.

I was fortunate to be able to discuss my project with a number of Mexican Americans who had wide-ranging knowledge about their own community and were able to approach the social world with considerable objectivity. These persons provided me with information regarding familial patterns beyond the groups I observed. They discussed patterns relating to both the extended and the conjugal family. Some of these persons were especially helpful in providing me with certain data on life-cycle rituals they remembered.

But these expert respondents did more than furnish me with data. They served as a significant check on my analysis of selected findings. For instance, early on I was criticized by several social scientists for insisting that working-class and professional women have different social identities.

I asked several Mexican American women who, because of their own social experiences, had knowledge of the lives of working- and professional-class women about the reactions of these critics, and they provided me with additional data that challenged the perspective of my critics.

My use of the objectifying interview is at odds with the views of, for example, Schutz (1978). He argued that the observations of social scientists are fundamentally different from the observations of persons in everyday life. My research experience indicates that he is incorrect.

Overall, the objectifying interview was still another method for "triangulating" data with respect to the family patterns I studied (Denzin 1989a). It served to provide me with certain data that supplemented data obtained from in-depth interviews and participant observation.

### The Researcher as Insider and Outsider

In 1972 Merton wrote a highly influential essay on researchers as insiders and as outsiders. While he did not adequately consider the issue of social power, which is central to research on majority/minority relations, he did raise issues worthy of serious attention.

As a Mexican American, I was an insider with respect to the Mexican American community; however, I have been educated in and have worked in a variety of Anglo environments. Like Merton, I believe that one should attempt to take the perspective of both insider and outsider, though this is difficult to achieve. Becker (1963:172-73) contends that one can adopt only one perspective at a time; both perspectives cannot be applied simultaneously. Nevertheless, if one cannot at least approximate Merton's orientation, one cannot study minority/majority relationships. In order for members of the minority community to adapt to the demands of the majority, they must constantly view their own perspective in the light of that taken by the majority. At the same time, it is difficult for many researchers in the majority sector to take the role of disadvantaged minorities (Williams 1989b).

Still, even as an insider, I encountered difficulties in conducting my research. Although I believe I established good rapport with most persons with whom I interacted, I was more an insider with respect to women than to men. I sought to take the role of husbands and attempted to understand how they defined their wives. At the same time, women spoke more freely to me, in part because women, in contrast to men, are more interested in familial issues. Moreover, I was unable to enter the world of men in certain contexts in the public sphere. Yet certain men spoke freely to me about the questions I addressed in my research.

Thus I have sought, as an ideal, to bridge the gap between insider and outsider, not only with respect to Mexican American married women and men but also with respect to Mexican Americans vis-à-vis members of the broader Anglo society.

## Analysis of the Data

Denzin (1989b), among others, has discussed some of the issues involved in analyzing and presenting qualitative data. For my purposes, three types of approaches can be distinguished. One is that exemplified by Lewis (1963), who sought to let respondents speak for themselves. At the other extreme are qualitative researchers who analyzed their findings with few, if any, quotations by respondents (e.g., Zurcher 1983; Stack 1974). I have followed a middle path between these two orientations. I would cite Rubin's (1976) work as one model for my study. But I have attempted to incorporate a more systematic theoretical perspective into the presentation of the findings than did Rubin.

For my analysis, I have selected quotations that I regard as typical of responses to the kinds of issues I am addressing. This is a judgment call on my part, but such judgment calls are, as McGrath et al. (1982) indicate, an integral part of the research process.

Ethical problems arise not only in the collection of data but also in the presentation of one's findings. I guaranteed anonymity to all my respondents. In some instances, I have been unable to quote directly certain statements, for some of these were so distinctive that it would be possible for others to identify the respondents. Or, in some instances, I have employed what Sjoberg and Nett (1968) refer to as "composite case." Here I have combined quotes from two persons. But I have done so only when they were similar and flowed naturally one into the other. The use of the "composite case" has been subjected to criticism; thus I have made limited use of it so as to sustain my pledge of anonymity.

Another difficulty I encountered has been analyzed in detail by Colvard (1967). He rightly reasons that researchers secure data often not as researchers per se but rather as friends of the respondents. I never made any secret of my research role. Nevertheless, persons with whom I interacted frequently told me about themselves or their activities because they viewed me as an acquaintance or friend, not as a researcher. I could not close my eyes and ears to what they did and said, but I have used these data with special care. They have typically served as background material that has helped me flesh out the information supplied to me in my more narrowly perceived role as a "researcher." At all times, I have attempted to treat respondents with the same concern and respect with which I would want to be treated.

# REFERENCES

Achor, S. 1978. *Mexican Americans in a Dallas Barrio*. Tucson, AZ: University of Arizona Press.

Alexander, J.C., B. Giesen, R. Munch, and N.J. Smelser. 1987. *The Micro-Macro Link*. Berkeley: University of California Press.

Aronson, E. 1988. *Social Animal*. 5th ed. New York: W.H. Freeman.

Atkinson, J. 1987. "Gender Roles in Marriage and the Family." *Journal of Family Issues* 8:5–41.

Baca Zinn, M. 1975. "Political Familism toward Sex Role Equality in Chicano Families." *Aztlan: International Journal of Chicano Studies* 6:13–27.

_____. 1976. "Chicanos: Power and Control in the Domestic Sphere." *De Colores* 2:19–31.

_____. 1980. "Employment and Education of Mexican American Women: The Interplay of Modernity and Ethnicity in Eight Families." *Harvard Educational Review* 50 (February):47–62.

_____. 1982. "Chicano Men and Masculinity." *Journal of Ethnic Studies* 10:29–44.

_____. 1984. "Mexican Heritage Women: A Bibliographic Essay." *Sage Race Relations Abstracts* 9:1–12.

Bailey, K.D. 1987. *Methods of Social Research*. 3rd ed. New York: Free Press.

Baldwin, J.D. 1988. "Habit, Emotion, and Self-Conscious Action." *Sociological Perspectives* 31:35–58.

Bean, F., and G. Swicegood. 1985. *Mexican American Fertility Patterns*. Austin: University of Texas Press.

Bean, F., and M. Tienda. 1987. *The Hispanic Population of the United States*. New York: Russell Sage Foundation.

Becker, H. 1963. *Outsiders*. New York: Free Press.

Bellah, R., R. Madsen, W. Sullivan, A. Swidler, and S. Tipton. 1985. *Habits of the Heart*. Berkeley: University of California Press.

Biddle, B.J. 1986. "Recent Developments in Role Theory." *Annual Review of Sociology* 12:67–92.

Billig, M., S. Condor, D. Edwards, M. Gane, D. Middleton, and A. Radley. 1988. *Ideological Dilemmas*. Newbury Park: Sage.

Blau, P. 1964. *Exchange and Power in Social Life*. New York: Wiley.

Blood, R. and D.M. Wolfe. 1960. *Husbands and Wives*. Glencoe, IL: Free Press.

Blumer, H. 1969. *Symbolic Interactionism*. Englewood Cliffs, NJ: Prentice-Hall.

Blumstein, P., and P. Schwartz. 1983. *American Couples*. New York: Morrow.

Cancian, F.M. 1987. *Love in America: Gender and Self-Development*. New York: Cambridge University Press.

Caplow, T., H.M. Bahr, B.A. Chadwich, R. Hill, and M.H. Williamson. 1982. *Middletown Families: Fifty Years of Change and Continuity*. New York: Bantam Books.

Chavez, J.R. 1984. *The Lost Land: The Chicano Image of the Southwest*. Albuquerque: University of New Mexico Press.

Clark, M. 1959. *Health in the Mexican-American Culture*. Berkeley: University of California Press.

160

Collins, R. 1988. *Sociology of Marriage & the Family: Gender, Love, and Property*. 2nd ed. Chicago: Nelson Hall.

_____. 1989. "Toward a Neo-Meadian Sociology of Mind." *Symbolic Interaction* 12:1–32.

Colvard, R. 1967. "Interaction and Identification in Reporting Field Research: A Critical Reconsideration of Protective Procedures." Pp. 319–58 in G. Sjoberg, ed., *Ethics, Politics, and Social Research*, Cambridge, MA: Schenkman.

Cook, K.S., and R.M. Emerson. 1978. "Power, Equity and Commitment in Exchange Networks." *American Sociological Review* 43:721–39.

Cromwell, R.E., R. Corrales, and P.M. Torsiello. 1973. "Normative Patterns of Marital Decision-Making Power and Influence in Mexico and the United States: A Partial Test of Resource and Ideology of Theory." *Journal of Comparative Family Studies* 4:177–96.

Cromwell, V.L., and R.E. Cromwell. 1978. "Perceived Dominance in Decision-Making and Conflict Resolution Among Anglo, Black and Chicano Couples." *Journal of Marriage and the Family* 40:749–59.

D'Antonio W., and J. Aldous, eds. 1983. *Families and Religions: Conflict and Change in Modern Society*. Beverly Hills: Sage.

Deegan, Mary Jo. In Press. "A Theory of American Drama and Ritual: Critical Dramaturgy." *American Ritual Dramas: Social Rules and Cultural Meanings*. Westport, CT: Greenwood Press.

De Leon, A. 1983. *They Called Them Greasers*. Austin: University of Texas Press.

Denzin, N.K. 1987. "Under the Influence of Time: Reading the Interactional Text." *Sociological Quarterly* 28:327–41.

_____. 1989a. *The Research Act*. 3rd ed. Englewood Cliffs, NJ: Prentice-Hall.

_____. 1989b. *Interpretive Interactionism*. Newbury Park: Sage.

Deutscher, I. 1973. *What We Say/What We Do*. Glenview, IL: Scott, Foresman.

Dubisch, J., ed. 1986. *Gender & Power in Rural Greece*. Princeton: Princeton University Press.

Durkheim, E. 1915. *The Elementary Forms of the Religious Life*. New York: Free Press.

Eliade, M. 1957. *The Sacred and the Profane*. New York: Harcourt, Brace and World.

Embree, J.F. 1939. *Suye Mura: A Japanese Village*. Chicago: University of Chicago Press.

Emerson, R.M. 1972. "Exchange Theory, Part I: A Psychological Basis for Social Exchange," and "Exchange Theory, Part II: Exchange Relations and Networks." Pp. 38–87 in J. Berger, M. Zeldith, Jr., and B. Anderson, eds., *Sociological Theories in Progress* Vol. 2. Boston: Houghton Mifflin.

Escobedo, T.H. 1980. "Are Hispanic Women in Higher Education the Nonexistent Minority?" *Educational Researcher* 9:7–12.

Farber, B. 1987. "The Future of the American Family." *Journal of Family Issues* 8:431–33.

Foa, E.B., and U.G. Foa. 1980. "Resource Theory: Interpersonal Behavior as Exchange." Pp. 77–94 in K.J. Gergen, M.S. Greenberg, and R.H. Willis, eds. *Social Exchange: Advances in Theory and Research*. New York: Plenum Press.

Foley, D.E., C. Mota, D.A. Post, and I. Lozano. 1988. *From Peones to Politicos: Class and Ethnicity in a South Texas Town 1900–1987*. Austin: University of Texas Press.

Fox-Genovese, E. 1988. *Within the Plantation Household: Black and White Women of the Old South*. Chapel Hill: University of North Carolina Press.

Fried, M.N., and M.H. Fried. 1980. *Transitions: Four Rituals in Eight Cultures*. New York: Norton.

Frisbie, P., F. Bean, and I. Eberstein. 1978. "Patterns of Marital Instability among Mexican Americans, Blacks, and Anglos." Pp. 143–63 in Bean and Frisbie, eds., *The Demography of Racial and Ethnic Groups*. New York: Academic Press.

Frisbie, W.P., and W. Kelly. 1985. "Marital Instability Trends among Mexican Americans as Compared to Blacks and Anglos." *Social Science Quarterly* 66:585–601.

Galbraith, J.K. 1971. *The New Industrial State*. 2nd ed. Boston: Houghton Mifflin.

Garfinkel, H. 1967. *Studies in Ethnomethodology*. Englewood Cliffs, NJ: Prentice-Hall.

Geertz, C. 1973. *The Interpretation of Cultures*. New York: Basic Books.

Gerson, K. 1985. *Hard Choices: How Women Decide about Work, Career, and Motherhood*. Berkeley: University of California Press.

Glenn, N.D. 1987. "Social Trends in the United States." *Public Opinion Quarterly* 51:109–26.

Goffman, E. 1959. *The Presentation of Self in Everyday Life*. Garden City, NY: Doubleday/Anchor.

_____. 1967. *Interaction Ritual*. Garden City, NY: Pantheon.

Goode, W.J. 1970. *World Revolution and Family Patterns*. New York: Free Press.

_____. 1973. *Explorations in Social Theory*. New York: Oxford University Press.

_____. 1983. "Why Men Resist." Pp. 201–18 in A. Skolnick and J. Skolnick, eds. *Family in Transition*. 4th ed. Boston: Little, Brown.

Gordon, M. 1964. *Assimilation in American Life*. New York: Oxford University Press.

Gouldner, A. 1960. "The Norm of Reciprocity." *American Sociological Review* 25:161–78.

Grebler, L., J. Moore, and R. Guzman. 1970. *The Mexican American People: The Nation's Second Largest Minority*. New York: Free Press.

Greeley, A.M. 1982. *Religion: A Secular Theory*. New York: Free Press.

Grider, S., and S.J. Jones. 1984. "The Cultural Legacy of Texas Cemetaries." *Texas Humanist* 6:34–39.

Griswold del Castillo, R. 1984. *La Familia: Chicano Families in the Urban Southwest, 1848 to the Present*. Notre Dame: University of Notre Dame Press.

Hawkes, G.R., and M. Taylor. 1975. "Power Structure in Mexican and Mexican-American Farm Labor Families." *Journal of Marriage and the Family* 37:807–11.

Hertz, R. 1986. *More Equal Than Others: Women and Men in Dual-Career Marriages*. Berkeley: University of California Press.

Hess, B.B., and M.M. Ferree, eds. 1987. *Analyzing Gender: A Handbook of Social Science Research*. Newbury Park: Sage.

Hinojosa Smith, R. 1988. "Sweet Fifteen." *Texas Monthly* 16:96–99.

Hobsbawm, E. 1983. "Introduction: Inventing Traditions." Pp.1–14 in E. Hobsbawm and T. Ranger, eds., *The Invention of Tradition*. New York: Cambridge University Press.

Hobsbawm, E., and T. Ranger, eds. 1983. *The Invention of Tradition*. New York: Cambridge University Press.

Horowitz, R. 1983. *Honor and the American Dream*. New Brunswick, NJ: Rutgers University Press.

Hutter, M. 1988. *The Changing Family: Comparative Perspectives*. 2nd ed. New York: Macmillan.

Jackson, J. 1986. *Los Mesteños*. College Station, TX: Texas A&M University Press.

Jordan, T. 1982. *Texas Graveyards: A Cultural Legacy*. Austin: University of Texas Press.

Keefe, S., A. Padilla, and M. Carlos. 1979. "The Mexican American Extended Family as an Emotional Support System." *Journal of the Society for Applied Anthropology* 38:144–52.

Keefe, S., and A. Padilla. 1987. *Chicano Ethnicity*. Albuquerque: University of New Mexico Press.

Kligman, G. 1988. *The Wedding of the Dead*. Berkeley: University of California Press.

Komarovsky, M. 1946. "Cultural Contradictions and Sex Roles." *American Journal of Sociology* 52:184–89.

_____. 1988. "The New Feminist Scholarship: Some Precursors and Polemics." *Journal of Marriage and the Family* 50:585–93.

Lal, B.B. 1986. "The 'Chicago School' of American Sociology, Symbolic Interactionism, and Race Relations Theory." Pp. 280–98 in J. Rex and D. Mason, eds, *Theories of Race and Ethnic Relations*. New York: Cambridge University Press.

Lasch, C. 1977. *Haven in a Heartless World*. New York: Basic Books.

———. 1978. *The Culture of Narcissism*. New York: Norton.

Lawe, C., and B. Lawe. 1980. "The Balancing Act: Coping Strategies for Emerging Family Lifestyles." Pp. 191–203 in F. Pepitone-Rockwell, ed., *Dual-Career Couples*. Beverly Hills: Sage.

Lee, G. 1982. *Family Structure and Interaction*. Minneapolis: University of Minnesota Press.

Lengermann, P.M., and J. Niebrugge-Brantley. 1988. "Contemporary Feminist Theory." Pp. 282–325 in G. Ritzer, *Contemporary Sociological Theory*, 2nd ed. New York: Knopf.

Lewis, O. 1963. *Children of Sanchez*. New York: Random House.

Lofland, J., and L.H. Lofland. 1984. *Analyzing Social Settings: A Guide to Qualitative Observation and Analysis*. Belmont, CA: Wadsworth.

Madsen, W. 1964. *The Mexican-Americans of South Texas*. New York: Holt, Rinehart, and Winston.

Mannheim, K. 1952. "The Problem of Generations." Pp. 262–322 in K. Mannheim, *Essays on the Sociology of Knowledge*. New York: Oxford University Press.

Marcus, G., and M. Fischer. 1986. *Anthropology as Cultural Critique*. Chicago: University of Chicago Press.

McCall, G. & J.L. Simmons. 1982. *Social Psychology: A Sociological Approach*. New York: Free Press.

McDonald, G.W. 1980. "Family Power: The Assessment of a Decade of Theory and Research, 1970–1979." *Journal of Marriage and the Family* 42:841–54.

McGrath, J., J. Martin, and R.A. Kulka. 1982. *Judgment Calls in Research*. Beverly Hills: Sage.

Mead, G.H. 1934. *Mind, Self and Society*. Chicago: University of Chicago Press.

———. 1938. *The Philosophy of the Act*. Chicago: University of Chicago Press.

Melville, M., ed. 1980. *Twice a Minority: Mexican American Women*. St. Louis: C.V. Mosby.

Merton, R.K. 1968. *Social Theory and Social Structure*. New York: Free Press.

———. 1972. "Insiders and Outsiders: A Chapter in the Sociology of Knowledge." *American Journal of Sociology* 78:9–47.

Mirandé, A. 1985. *The Chicano Experience: An Alternative Perspective*. Notre Dame: University of Notre Dame Press.

Mirandé, A., and E. Enríquez. 1979. *La Chicana*. Chicago: University of Chicago Press.

Molm, L.D. 1987. "Power-Dependence Theory: Power Processes and Negative Outcomes." Pp. 171–98 in E.J. Lawler and B. Markovsky, eds., *Advances in Group Processes* Vol. 4. Greenwich: JAI Press.

Montejano, D. 1987. *Anglos and Mexicans in the Making of Texas, 1836–1986*. Austin: University of Texas Press.

Montiel, M. 1970. "The Social Science Myth of the Mexican American Family." *El Grito: A Journal of Contemporary Mexican American Thought* 3:56–63.

Moore, J. 1970. "The Death Culture of Mexico and Mexican-Americans." *Omega* 1:271–91.

———. 1976. *Mexican Americans*. Englewood Cliffs, NJ: Prentice-Hall.

Moschetti, G.J. 1979. "The Christmas Potlatch: Refinement on the Sociological Interpretation of Gift Exchange." *Sociological Focus* 12:1–7.

Murguia, E. 1982. *Chicano Intermarriage*. San Antonio, TX: Trinity University Press.

Nicholson, L.J. 1986. *Gender and History*. New York: Columbia University Press.

Paredes, A. 1958. *With His Pistol in His Hand*. Austin: University of Texas Press.

Paredes, A. 1977. "On Ethnographic Work among Minority Groups." *New Scholar* 6:1–32.

Parsons, T. 1937. *The Structure of Social Action*. New York: Free Press.

Parsons, T., and R.F. Bales. 1955. *Family, Socialization and Interaction Process*. New York: Free Press.

Payne, H.C. 1984. "The Ritual Question and Modernizing Society, 1800–1945 – A Schema for a History." *Historical Reflections/Reflexions and Historiques* 11:403-32.

Pinkerton, J. 1988. "Day of the Dead Is Observed with Modern Celebration." *Austin American-Statesman*.

Popenoe, D. 1988. *Disturbing the Nest*. New York: Aldine De Gruyter.

Queen, S.A., R.W. Habenstein, and J.S. Quadagno. 1985. *The Family in Various Cultures*. New York: Harper & Row.

Rodriguez, R. 1982. *Hunger of Memory*. New York: Bantam Books.

Roof, W.C. 1985. "The Study of Social Change in Religion." Pp. 75–89 in P.E. Hammond, ed., *The Sacred in a Secular Age*. Berkeley: University of California Press.

Rosaldo, M.Z. 1974. "Woman, Culture, and Society: A Theoretical Overview." Pp. 17–42 in M.Z. Rosaldo and L. Lamphere, eds., *Woman, Culture, & Society*. Stanford: Stanford University Press.

Rubel, A. 1966. *Across the Tracks: Mexican-Americans in a Texas City*. Austin: University of Texas Press.

Rubin, D.C., ed. 1986. *Autobiographical Memory*. New York: Cambridge University Press.

Rubin, L.B. 1976. *Worlds of Pain*. New York: Basic Books.

Ruiz, V.L. 1987. *Cannery Women/Cannery Lives*. Albuquerque: University of New Mexico Press.

Safilios-Rothschild, C. 1969. "Family Sociology or Wives' Family Sociology? A Cross-Cultural Examination of Decision-Making." *Journal of Marriage and the Family* 31:290–301.

Sanford, A.J. 1987. *The Mind of Man*. New Haven: Yale University Press.

San Miguel, G, Jr. 1987. *"Let All of Them Take Heed." Mexican Americans and the Campaign for Educational Equality in Texas, 1910–1981*. Austin: University of Texas Press.

Scanzoni, J., and M. Szinovacz. 1980. *Family Decision-Making*. Beverly Hills: Sage.

Schultz, T., E. Murguia, and S.K. Hoppe. 1988. "Gender Role Orientations among Three Generations of Mexican American Women." Pp. 87–100 in *The 1988 Victoria College Social Sciences Symposium*. Victoria, TX: Victoria College Press.

Schutz, A. 1978. *The Theory of Social Action: The Correspondence of Alfred Schutz and Talcott Parsons*. Edited by Richard Grathoff. Bloomington: Indiana University Press.

Sena-Rivera, J. 1979. "Extended Kinship in the United States: Competing Models and the Case of La Familia Chicana." *Journal of Marriage and the Family* 41:121-29.

Shapiro, V. 1986. *Women in American Society*. Palo Alto: Mayfield.

Sjoberg, G., and R. Nett. 1968. *A Methodology for Social Research*. New York: Harper & Row.

Skolnick, A.S. 1987. *The Intimate Environment*. 4th ed. Boston: Little, Brown.

Smith, C.W. 1982. "On the Sociology of Mind." Pp. 221–28 in P. Secord, ed., *Explaining Human Behavior*. Beverly Hills: Sage.

Smith, R.E., ed. 1979. *The Subtle Revolution*. Washington, DC: Urban Institute.

Smith, R.J., and E.L. Wiswell. 1982. *The Women of Suye Mura*. Chicago: University of Chicago Press.

Snow, D.A., L.A. Zurcher, and G. Sjoberg. 1982. "Interviewing by Comment: An Adjunct to the Direct Question." *Qualitative Sociology* 5:385-411.

Stack, C. 1974. *All Our Kin*. New York: Harper & Row.

Staples, R., and A. Mirandé. 1980. "Racial and Cultural Variations among American Families: A Decennial Review of the Literature on Minority Families." *Journal of Marriage and the Family* 42:157-73.

Strauss, A. 1978. *Negotiations: Varieties, Contexts, Processes, and Social Order*. San Francisco: Jossey-Bass.

Stryker, S. 1980. *Symbolic Interaction: A Social Structural Version*. Menlo Park, CA: Benjamin Cummings.

Stryker, S., and A. Statham. 1985. "Symbolic Interaction and Role Theory." Pp. 311–78 in G. Lindzey and E. Aronson, eds., *The Handbook of Social Psychology* Vol. 1. 3rd ed. New York: Random House.

Sussman, M.B., ed. 1968. *Sourcebook in Marriage and the Family*. Boston: Houghton Mifflin.

Terkel, S. 1988. *The Great Divide*. New York: Pantheon.

Thurow, L.C. 1983. *Dangerous Currents*. New York: Random House.

Tienda M., and V. Ortiz. 1986. "Hispanicity and the 1980 Census." *Social Science Quarterly* 67:3–20.

Turner, R. 1962. "Role Taking: Process Versus Conformity." Pp. 20–39 in A. Rose, ed., *Human Behavior and Social Processes*. London: Routledge and Kegan Paul.

_____. 1970. *Family Interaction*. New York: Wiley.

_____. 1976. "The Real Self: From Institution to Impulse." *American Journal of Sociology* 81:989–1016.

_____. 1985. "Unanswered Questions in the Convergence Between Structuralist and Interactionist Role Theories." Pp. 22–36 in H.J. Helle and S.N. Eisenstadt, eds., *Micro-Sociological Theory Perspectives on Sociological Theory* Vol. 2. Beverly Hills: Sage.

Turner, R.H, and N. Shosid. 1976. "Ambiguity and Interchangeability in Role Attribution: The Effect of Alter's Response." *American Sociological Review* 41:993–1006.

U.S. Bureau of the Census. 1983a. "Census Tracts, Austin, Texas, SMSA, PHC80-2-80." In *Census of Population and Housing, 1980*. Washington, DC: U.S. Government Printing Office.

_____. 1983b. "Census Tracts, Corpus Christi, Texas, SMSA, PHC80-2-129." In *Census of Population and Housing, 1980*. Washington, DC: U.S. Government Printing Office.

_____. 1983c. "General Social and Economic Characteristics," Part 45, TEXAS PC80-1-C45. In *1980 Census of Population*. Vol. 1, Chap. 3.

Valle, J.R. 1974. "Amistad-Compadrazgo as an Indigenous Network Compared to the Urban Mental Health Network." Unpublished dissertation, University of Southern California.

Van Gennep, A. 1960. *The Rites of Passage*. Chicago: University of Chicago Press.

Vaughan, T.R., and G. Sjoberg. 1984. "The Individual and Bureaucracy: An Alternative Meadian Interpretation." *Journal of Applied Behavioral Science* 20:57–69.

Waugh, J.N. 1988. *The Silver Cradle: Las Posadas, Los Pastores, and Other Mexican American Traditions*. Austin: University of Texas Press. Originally published in 1955.

Wax, R. 1952. "Field Methods and Techniques: Reciprocity as a Field Technique." *Human Organization* 11:34–37.

Weber, D.J. 1981. "Failure of a Frontier Institution: The Secular Church in the Borderlands under Independent Mexico." *The Western Historical Quarterly* 13:125–43.

Weigert, A.J. 1983. "Identity: Its Emergence within Sociological Psychology." *Symbolic Interaction* 6:183–206.

Weiner, A. 1976. *Women of Value, Men of Renown*. Austin: University of Texas Press.

Whyte, W.F. 1955. *Street Corner Society*. 2nd ed. Chicago: University of Chicago Press.

_____. 1984. *Learning from the Field*. Beverly Hills: Sage.

Williams, N. 1987. "Changes in Funeral Patterns and Gender Roles among Mexican Americans." Pp. 197–217 in V.L. Ruiz and S. Tiano, eds., *Women on the U.S.-Mexico Border: Responses to Change*. Boston: Allen & Unwin.

_____. 1988. "Role Making among Married Mexican American Women: Issues of Class and Ethnicity." *Journal of Applied Behavioral Science* 24:203–17.

_____. 1989a. "Theoretical and Methodological Issues in the Study of Role Making." In N. Denzin, ed., *Studies in Symbolic Interaction: A Research Annual* Vol. 10. Greenwich: JAI Press.

_____. 1989b. "Role Taking and the Study of Majority/Minority Relationships." *Journal of Applied Behavioral Science* 25.

Williams, N., G. Sjoberg, and A.F. Sjoberg. 1983. "The Bureaucratic Personality: A Second Look." Pp. 173-89, in W.B. Littrell, G. Sjoberg, and L.A. Zurcher, eds., *Bureaucracy as a Social Problem*. Greenwich, CT: JAI Press.

Wilson, B.R. 1966. *Religion in Secular Society: A Sociological Comment*. London: Watts.

Wolf, E.R., and E.C. Hansen. 1972. *The Human Condition in Latin America*. New York: Oxford University Press.

Wolf, E.R. 1982. *Europe and the People without History*. Berkeley: University of California Press.

Wrong, D.H. 1979. *Power: Its Forms, Bases and Uses*. New York: Harper & Row.

Ybarra, L. 1977. "Conjugal Role Relationships in the Chicano Family." Unpublished dissertation, University of California, Berkeley.

_____. 1982. "When Wives Work: The Impact on the Chicano Family." *Journal of Marriage and the Family* 44:169-78.

Zavella, P. 1987. *Women's Work and Chicano Families*. Ithaca, NY: Cornell University Press.

Zurcher, L.A. 1977. *The Mutable Self: A Self-Concept for Social Change*. Beverly Hills: Sage.

_____. 1983. *Social Roles: Conformity, Conflict and Creativity*. Beverly Hills: Sage.

_____. 1986a. "The Future of the Reservist: A Case of Constructive Brokering." Pp. 221-53 in L. Zurcher, M. Boykin, and H. Merritt, eds., *Citizen-Sailors in a Changing Society: Policy Issues for Manning the United States Naval Reserve*. New York: Greenwood Press.

_____. 1986b. "The Bureaucratizing of Impulse: Self-Conception in the 1980's." *Symbolic Interaction* 9:169-78.

# Index

Achor, S., 26, 27
Aldous, J., 17, 80
assimilation
  critique of assimilation model, 6–7,
    43, 144–151
  perspective of, 145, 151

Baca Zinn, M., 2, 16
Bailey, K.D., 154
baptismal ceremony (see also com-
    padrazgo)
  bureaucratization of, 48–50
  professional class, 65–70
  traditional patterns, 23–27
  working class, 44–51
Bean, F., 3, 5, 16, 151
Bellah, R., 146
Biddle, B.J., 13, 108
Blau, P., 140
Blood, R., 11, 83, 97, 151
Blumer, H., 12, 20, 141, 142, 151
Blumstein, P., 4–5, 6
Bureaucracy
  bureaucratization, 5, 40, 44, 55,
    57–58, 81, 138, 148
  emotions, 57–59
  federal and governmental, 2, 142

Cancian, F.M., 146
Catholicism (see also religion), 22, 31–32,
    36
  neglect of Mexican American culture,
    50, 72
Chavez, J.R., 3, 21
Chicano (see also Mexican American), 136
  definition of, 2, 16–17
choice of friends, 104–105, 130–132
Clark, M., 1, 26, 27
collective memory (see social memory)
Collins, R., 14, 90, 109, 141, 142, 151
compadrazgo (see also baptismal
    ceremony)

fictive kinship, 24, 26, 38, 41, 44, 47,
    50, 63, 65, 70, 138
  professional class, 65–70
  traditional patterns of, 23–27
  vertical, 26
  working class, 44–51
comadre (co-mother) (see also baptismal
    ceremony), 24, 25–26, 33, 36,
    46–47, 67
compadre (co-father) (see also baptismal
    ceremony), 24, 25–26, 46–47, 66, 67
conjugal relationships (see also decision
    making), 1, 9–11, 12, 19, 39, 41,
    45, 64, 70, 77, 83–84, 137
contradictory role expectations, 14, 23,
    96, 118, 140, 143–144
Cook, K.S., 140, 141
Cromwell, R.E., 11, 83, 116
Cromwell, V.L., 11, 116

D'Antonio, W., 17, 80
Day of the Dead (see also funerals), 38,
    40, 62–63, 80, 82
decision making, 10, 11, 138–139
  egalitarianism, 11, 83, 116, 118, 135,
    139
  negotiated order, 93, 129, 134, 135,
    143
  professional class, 123–134
    perception of change, 111–113
    sex-role expectations, 113–115
    specific decision-making areas,
      124–134
  working class, 96–108
    perception of change, 84–87
    sex-role expectations, 87–90
    specific decision making areas,
      97–108
Deegan, M.J., 20
De Leon, A., 16
Denzin, N.K., 126, 152, 158, 159
Deutscher, I., 8, 87, 157

167

disciplining of children, 105–107, 132–134
discrimination, 4, 14, 96, 122–123, 139, 145
Durkheim, E., 10, 18–19, 40, 77, 141

egalitarianism (see decision making)
Eliade, M., 18, 20, 137
Embree, J.F., 16
Emerson, R.M., 140, 141
Enriquez, E., 16
Escobedo, T.H., 151
esquela
    copy of, 34
    meaning of, 33, 56
    professional class, 74
    traditional patterns, 33–34
    working class, 56
ethical issues (see research procedures)
ethnicity, 11, 40, 72, 73, 95, 96, 122, 123, 136, 139, 144–148
    diversity, 150
exchange theory, 12, 83, 84, 97, 111, 123, 124, 140–141, 151
extended family, 1, 9–10, 25, 36, 38, 41, 45, 54–55, 78, 8l, 137–138, 142
    changes in professional class, 64, 70, 73, 77, 78, 79
    changes in traditional patterns, 32, 54, 64, 73
    changes in working class, 51, 60, 63

Farber, B., 149
fatalism, 22
Ferree, M.M., 151
fictive kinship (see compadrazgo)
Fischer, M., 12
Foley, D.E., 21, 39
Fox-Genovese, E., 147
Fried, M.H., 19
Fried, M.N., 19
funerals
    changing patterns, 56–63
    Day of the Dead, 38, 40, 62–63, 80, 82
    emotions, 35, 36–38, 57–59, 61, 75, 77
    mourning of, 37, 61–62, 79–80, 91
    novenarios, 37, 61, 79
    professional class, 74–80
    religious meaning, 36, 58, 75–77
    traditional patterns, 33–38, 59
    working class, 56–63

Garfinkel, H., 129
Geertz, C., 10
generational differences, 4, 42–43, 52, 63, 74, 84–85, 110, 138, 143, 149
Gerson, K., 84, 89
Glenn, N.D., 6
godparents (see baptismal ceremony, madrina, and padrino)
Goffman, E., 20, 93
Goode, W.J., 5, 95, 96, 144, 148
Gordon, M., 144
Gouldner, A., 141
Grebler, L., 10, 24, 26, 130
Greeley, A.M., 43, 65
Griswold del Castillo, 16
Guadalupe Hidalgo, Treaty of, 2–3, 151

Hansen, E., 26
Hawkes, G.R., 11, 83
Hertz, R., 84, 110, 122
Hess, B.B., 151
Hinojosa Smith, R., 39, 82
Horowitz, R., 2, 16

industrialization, 5, 40, 81, 138
interview procedures (see research procedures)

Jackson, J., 21, 151

Keefe, S., 4, 10, 63, 64
Komarovsky, M., 96, 109

la familia (see extended family)
Lasch, C., 6, 142, 146
Lee, G., 109
Lengermann, P.M., 147
life-cycle rituals (see also baptismal ceremony, marriage rite, and funerals), 9–10, 15, 18, 40, 41, 137
    professional class, 65–80
    religious significance, 44, 80
    sacred time, 20, 43, 65, 67, 137
    secular time, 20, 43, 65, 80, 82
    social significance of, 19–20
    traditional patterns, 42, 72, 82
    working class, 44–63
Lofland, J., 8, 152
Lofland, L.H., 8, 152

McCall, G., 14, 90, 121, 142
McDonald, G.W., 84, 97, 111
McGrath, J., 159
machismo (male dominance), 2, 17, 29, 39, 83
madrina (godmother) (see also baptismal ceremony), 24, 25, 26, 69, 72
Madsen, W., 1-2, 8, 11, 22, 83, 138
management of finances, 98-99, 124-126
Mannheim, K., 63
Marcus, G., 12
marriage rite
    professional class, 70-74
    traditional patterns, 27-33
    working class, 51-56
Mead, G.H., 12, 108, 141, 142
Melville, M., 95
men's roles
    professional class, 117-121, 123
    traditional patterns, 28-29, 33, 35-38
    working class, 88-91
Merton, R., 141, 158
Mexican American (see also Chicano)
    different from Anglos, 4, 7, 20-21, 81-82, 145-146, 149-150
    different from Mexican nationals, 2, 3-4, 16-17, 20-21
    variations within, 4, 7, 27-28
Mirandé, A., 2, 16
Montejano, D., 6
Montiel, M., 16
Moore, J., 2
Murguia, E., 16

nuclear family, 9, 32, 38, 60, 63, 72

Ortiz, V., 17

Padilla, A., 4, 10, 63, 64
padrino (godfather) (see also baptismal ceremony), 24, 26
Paredes, A., 1-2, 21
Parsons, T., 113, 141
participant observation (see research procedures)
Popenoe, D., 5, 148
portador (intermediary)
    changing patterns, 52, 70-71
    definition of, 27-28
    function of, 27-29, 51-52
    traditional patterns, 27-29, 51-52, 70-71

private sphere (see also decision making), 2, 16, 18, 87, 99, 123
professional class, 64-82, 110-135
    similar to business/professional, 7, 64, 110, 152
public sphere (see also decision making), 2, 11, 16, 18, 30, 91, 96, 99, 101, 116, 117, 123, 158
purchase of a car, 99-101, 126-128
purchase of furniture, 102-104, 128-130

quinceañera, 17, 24, 27, 39, 82

religion
    changing patterns, 44, 53-54, 62, 67-70, 80-81
    generalized belief system, 44, 58, 67, 76, 80-81
    importance in marriage ceremony, 31-32, 52-53, 73
    nature of, 43-44
    Roman Catholicism, 22, 31-32, 44, 47-48
    sacred religious tradition, 20
research procedures
    ethical issues, 159
    in-depth interviews, 7, 11, 14, 152-156
    insider/outsider, 158-159
    nature of sample, 7-8, 21, 152-156
    objectifying interview, 152, 157-158
    participant observation, 7, 8, 11, 14, 156-157
research sites
    Austin, 7-8, 152-158
    Corpus Christi, 7-8, 152-158
    Kingsville region, 8, 17, 153-158
respect, 25, 37, 47, 86
responsibility for house repairs, 101-102, 128
rites of passage (see life-cycle rituals)
rituals (see life-cycle rituals)
Rodriguez, R., 145
role making (see also decision making), 10-11, 13, 84, 108, 139
    different from role taking, 89-90, 108
    professional class, 115-123, 126
        constraints on, 117, 121-123
        role making process, 115-116, 122
        role making types, 116-121
    theoretical implications, 89-90, 108, 144

working class, 89–90
    resistance to, 95–96
    role making types, 92–95, 108, 132
    specific patterns, 90–95
role taking (see also decision making)
    different from role making, 89–90,
        108
Roof, W.C., 43
Rosaldo, M.Z., 2
Rubel, A., 1–2, 4, 8, 11, 17, 22, 24, 26,
    83, 138
Rubin, L., 14, 123, 159
Ruiz, V.L., 16

sample (see research procedures)
San Miguel, G., 145
Schultz, T.E., 81, 151
Schwartz, P., 4–5, 6
Sena-Rivera, J., 10, 63, 64
Shosid, N., 89
Simmons, J.L., 14, 90, 121, 142
sisterhood, 146–148
Sjoberg, G., 14, 90, 142, 151, 157, 159
Smith, C.W., 14, 90
Smith, R.J., 2, 16
Snow, D., 154
social identity (see also role making)
    professional class, 122–123, 135, 139
    working class, 91–95, 107–108, 116,
        135, 139
social memory, 13, 20, 21, 65, 67, 71, 74,
    81, 90, 95, 110, 117, 138, 143–144,
    154
social mind, 12, 13–14, 20, 81, 90, 97,
    109, 140, 142, 144
social roles (see contradictory role
    expectations and decision making)
social self, 12, 13–14, 20, 81, 90, 140, 142,
    144, 145–146
Spanish language, 3, 69
Stack, C., 14, 159
Staples, R., 16
Statham, A., 91

stereotypes, 1–2, 16, 23, 112, 138–139
    critique of, 1–2, 16
Stryker, S., 91, 142, 151
subtle revolution, 5–6
symbolic interaction, 12–14, 19–20, 97,
    126, 136
    revisions in, 12–14, 140–142

Taylor, M., 11, 83
Tienda, M., 3, 5, 16, 17
tradition (see all life-cycle rituals)
    among Mexican Americans, 20–22
    nature of, 9–10, 13, 39
Turner, R., 6, 13, 89, 90, 108, 145–146
twice a minority (see also women), 11–12,
    14, 15, 95, 96, 122, 139, 146, 149

U.S. Bureau of the Census, 7, 16, 17
urbanization, 5, 40, 58, 81, 130, 138, 148

van Gennep, A., 18
Vaughan, T.R., 14, 90, 142, 151

Weiner, A., 16
Whyte, W.F., 152, 157
Williams, N., 108, 141, 148, 151, 158
Wiswell, E.L., 2, 16
Wolf, E.R., 21, 26
Wolfe, D.M., 11, 83, 97, 151
women's movement, 43, 146–147
women's roles (see also decision making,
        life-cycle rituals, role making, and
        twice a minority)
    changing of, 61–62, 83–109, 110–135
    good/bad image, 23, 30
    professional class, 110–135
    traditional patterns, 2, 24–39
    working class, 83–109

Ybarra, L., 11, 83, 116

Zavella, P., 1, 11, 16, 83
Zurcher, L.A., 6, 8, 14, 89, 96, 120,
    145–146, 159